THE DIARY OF
A POOR SUFFOLK WOODMAN

The Diary of a poor Suffolk woodman

The Journal written in the
Thorpe Morieux Prayer Book
by William Scarfe
1827–1842

*Edited by Pip & Joy Wright
and Léonie Robinson*

POPPYLAND
PUBLISHING

Copyright © 2004 Pip & Joy Wright & Léonie Robinson

ISBN 0 946148 67 8

Published by
Poppyland Publishing
Cromer, Norfolk

Many Poppyland Publishing titles now have supplementary materials
which you can find by visiting <www.poppyland.co.uk> and clicking on the
'Support and Resources' button.

Front cover picture by Daniel Wright

Printed by Printing Services (Norwich) Ltd

*Bark strippers at work, from the photo collection belonging to the Museum of East
Anglian Life at Stowmarket*

Foreword

by Léonie Robinson

FROM MY EARLIEST CHILDHOOD, I can remember being told of an ancestor, William Scarfe, who, being one of the few in his village who could read and write, had kept a journal in the margins of a Prayer Book.

The book was then in the care of my grandmother, who on high days and holidays would produce it and pass it around. She was born Lois Hilda Scarfe and came from Thorpe Morieux in Suffolk. Some fifteen years ago, when I began to take an interest in my family history, I was given the book to keep, and until two years ago, that is just what I did with it. It was kept in a box, only occasionally looked at. Then, Pip Wright gave me a copy of a historical novel he had written. Reading it prompted me to start transcribing the words of William Scarfe.

Acknowledgements

THANKS AND ACKNOWLEDGEMENT are due to a number of people, without whose help, the publication of this book would not have been possible. These people include the staff of the Suffolk Record Offices at Bury St Edmunds and Ipswich; Dr Cockayne; John Squirrel; Gerald Morley; Donald Sewell; Tony Webster; the Buckmaster family; Barry and Julia Gooch; Joan Smith; Mrs G. Pilling; Nic Portway; Brian Harrison; Roger Neyland; Daniel Wright; Malcolm Marjoram; the Churchwardens and P.C.C. of Felsham; Felsham Parish Council. It also seems fair to recognise the contribution of the 19th century historian, John Glyde, to our researches.

Contents

Introduction   9

A note on the transcription of the diary   16

The Journal   17

Appendices:

    The Scarfe family in Felsham   162

    The Rectors of Thorpe Morieux   166

    Education at the time of William Scarfe   171

    The causes of death in the 19th century   173

    Fairs at the time of William Scarfe   174

    Crime in the early 1800s   177

Index   181

THE BOOK
COMMON PRAYER,
AND ADMINISTRATION
OF
The Sacraments
AND OTHER
RITES AND CEREMONIES OF THE CHURCH,
ACCORDING TO THE USE OF THE
United Church of England and Ireland;
TOGETHER WITH
THE PSALTER
OR
PSALMS OF DAVID,
POINTED AS THEY ARE TO BE SUNG OR
SAID IN CHURCHES.

Stereotype Edition.

CAMBRIDGE:

PRINTED BY J. SMITH, PRINTER TO THE UNIVERSITY;

FOR THE SOCIETY FOR PROMOTING CHRISTIAN KNOWLEDGE,

Sold by F. C. & J. RIVINGTON, Booksellers to the Society, London.

1823

Pica 8vo.   Cum Privilegio.   Price 3s. 0d.

Introduction

by Pip & Joy Wright

WHEN WE FIRST SAW the Thorpe Morieux Prayer Book, we instantly realised here was a very special document. We had read plenty of rich men's diaries, but here were the words of a working man in the early nineteenth century. Léonie began, painstakingly, transcribing the work. As she didn't have a computer printer, she passed us her transcriptions day by day, page by page, and we worked together reconstructing the times of William Scarfe. We always knew this was a diary that deserved a wider audience. It enables us to step into a world relating not merely to Thorpe Morieux, nor just to Suffolk. Laid bare is the life of a simple working man of his time.

Few of William Scarfe's class could write well enough to produce, as he did, more than fifteen years of a journal. Now, over 150 years later, we are privileged to be able to share the world of William Scarfe and enjoy the social history of the 1830s through his own words.

Undoubtedly, the only surviving record of many of the events described here is to be found within these pages.

Some time around the beginning of 1827, Reverend Thomas Thomas Harrison, Rector of Thorpe Morieux in Suffolk, gave a

Two paintings of Thorpe Morieux from the time of
William Scarfe, painted by W. Chandler

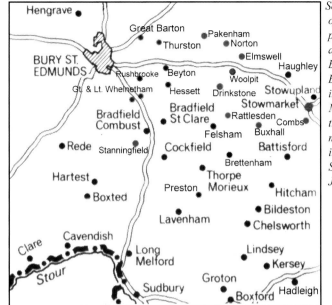

Some of the parishes around Bury St. Edmunds in Suffolk. Many of these are mentioned in William Scarfe's Journal.

Thorpe Morieux lies just three miles from Lavenham and nine miles from Bury St. Edmunds in the Cosford Hundred of West Suffolk.

book of Common Prayer to William Scarfe, a woodman in his parish. We can only surmise how this simple countryman had learned to read and write. The date of the book's publication was 1823, the same date Thomas Harrison had

Scarfe is a good name for a woodman – the word means a kind of overlapping joint like that shown in this barrel hoop.

acquired the living of what had been his uncle's parish before him. Perhaps he had recognised the intelligence and desire to learn of William Scarfe and his wife Mary. One thing is certain. Shortly after acquiring the book, William began to write on the blank pages at the front and back.

He first entered family details; births, deaths and marriages, such as are found in many old family Bibles. But he didn't stop there. Anxious to chronicle the important events in his life and lacking other paper, with ink and quill he proceeded to fill the margins of the prayer book with the history of the next fifteen years or more. The entries are in no obvious order, but most carry a date. They are written, apparently mostly in the same hand, at the top, bottom and sides of most pages. After about 1842, they become less frequent. One entry for that year says merely, 'Wm Scarfe Lost his sterngth'.

His spelling was erratic, often phonetic, and betrays a strong Suffolk accent. However, this is a rare glimpse into the life of a relatively poor man in the early years of the nineteenth century. So many diaries and journals of this time were written by the rich and educated. They concern themselves with hunting, feasting and travelling. William Scarfe's journal offers an alternative view of the time. It tells of the weather, his work as a woodman, his friends and neighbours and the things that seemed important to him.

The writing of this journal was almost certainly the work of William Scarfe Senior (1777–1848), but he did have a son of the same name. William Scarfe Junior also learned to read and write but at the time of his first marriage in 1825 he signed the register with a cross. In 1836 when he married for the second time, he signed his own name. Although most of the diary is written in the third person, it appears to be the work of William Scarfe the father, who makes it clear that his grandson John should be the book's keeper after his death. We are able to trace the succession of the book's keepers, an unbroken line, which has allowed us this unique insight into the world of William Scarfe of Thorpe Morieux.

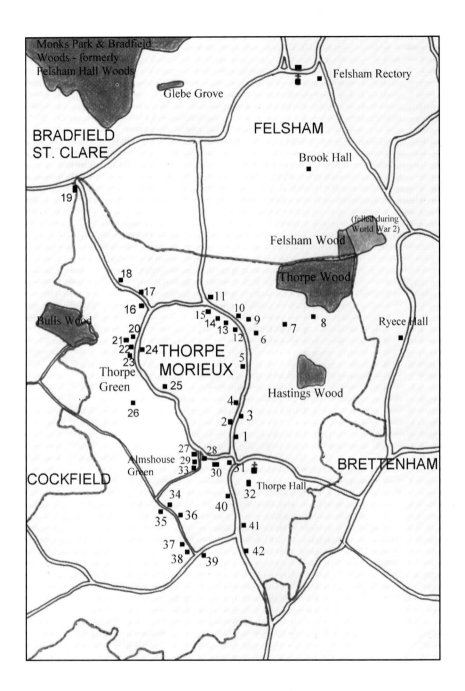

Monks Park & Bradfield
Woods - formerly
Felsham Hall Woods

Glebe Grove

Felsham Rectory

BRADFIELD
ST. CLARE

FELSHAM

Brook Hall

19

(felled during
World War 2)

Felsham Wood

Thorpe Wood

18

17

11

Bulls Wood

16

15   10
14   9
13
12   6
5

Ryece Hall

20

21
22
23
24 THORPE
MORIEUX

7   8

Thorpe
Green

26

25

4

Hastings Wood

2   3

1

27   28
Almshouse   29
Green   33   30

31

COCKFIELD

BRETTENHAM

32   Thorpe Hall

34

40

35   36

41

37
38   39

42

No.	Name		No.	Name	
1	William North	Wheelwright	22	George Long	
2	John Palmer		23	James Last	(Thorpe Green Farm)
3	William Scarfe Snr. & Jnr.	Woodmen (Moat Farm Cottage)	24	Hunt & others	
4	Robert Chenery	(Moat Farm)	25	Elizabeth Mudd	(Water Hall)
5	Robert Osborne		26	Benjamin Smith	
6	George Boggis & others		27	Bixby Gould	Parish Clerk
7	William Dyer	(Valley Farm, now called Grove Farm)	28	John Offord	
8	William Lister		29	John Green & others	
9	Charles Scott	(Folly Farm)	30	Rev. Thomas Thos. Harrison	Rector
10	Joseph Aves	Shoemaker	31	John Manning	
11	John Mannington	Farmer	32	Robert Mumford	Farm Steward (Thorpe Hall)
12	Edward Crick & others		33	George Howard & others	
13	North		34	Elizabeth Smith	
14	Owner: Charles Scott	(Sparkes Farm)	35	Bridget Hustler	(The Grange)
15	Jeremiah Craske	(Home Farm)	36	Thomas Stearn	(Birds Farm)
16	William Newson	(Reads Farm, now Newsons Farm)	37	Samuel Rush	Blacksmith
17	George Howe & others		38	William Hoddy	
18	Thomas Scott	(Elm Tree Farm)	39	John Stearn	(Hill Farm)
19	Clarke & others	(The Stone)	40	James Saddler	
20	Francis Lister		41	Richard Offord	(The Wash)
21	James Howard Sam Howard		42	Robert Allerson	

The map opposite is based on the Tithe Map of 1843, and shows the properties occupied by William Scarfe and his neighbours. The table above is an attempt, using the Tithe Apportionment and 1841 census, to indicate the occupiers of these properties at that time.

A note on the transcription of the diary

We have tried to be as faithful as possible in transcribing what was written in the prayer book. However, arriving at the finished result has required a measure of compromise and interpretation.

The writer would begin writing in one place and finish earlier on the page. For the sake of clarity, we have written his words in the order we believe he intended them to be read.

Another problem has been his use of the letters 'p' and 'f'. At first glance, he seems to spell his name 'Scarpe', as it tends to be written in early parish records. It may be that his name was still known as 'Scarpe'. However, whenever he writes 'f' followed by the letter 'e' it looks like a 'p' as in the word 'wife'. Most contemporary documents write 'Scarfe', as the name is generally spelt today, and it is that spelling we have opted for.

His use of the long 's' has been modernised, so that 'Heſset' becomes 'Hesset'.

We have tried to be as faithful as possible as regards upper and lower case letters, but a large measure of disagreement still exists between us, especially regarding the letters 'f', 't' and 'm'.

It was not uncommon to find two different spellings of the same word in the same sentence – and he almost never punctuated anything. We have left things as he wrote them.

The Journal
of William Scarfe

All five of William Scarfe's grandsons became woodmen or hurdle-makers. This is an early photograph of one of them, probably John, who took charge of the prayer book on his grandfather's death, and continued to live and work in Thorpe Morieux where his grandfather and father had before him.

A Count of Popel that Died in year of 1827

(The diary begins with a list of burials, then expands into other items. However, deaths continue to feature large in William Scarfe's journal.)

1827 Jan 6   Jan 6 1827 Died the Duke of york 20 minutes after 9 was Bured a Winsor

1827 Mar 30   Thomas Aves Died *(aged 77)*

1827 Apr 5   *(Thomas Aves)* was Bured at Bradfield St Cleare was Carred from Thorpe

             (From the centre of Thorpe to Bradfield St Clare Church is about two and a half miles.)

St. Clare's Church, Bradfield St. Clare

1827 Apr 19   young Norman fell of Cockfield Stepel he Died
from the fall he was stopping of holes in the Stepel
the Rope Brock The Fournoon he cut his Name and
age in the stepel the afternoon fell Down and Died

*(William Norman, aged 18, was buried at Cockfield, April
23rd 1827. The Bury Post for 25th April 1827 records that
'On Friday last, an inquisition was taken by John Wayman,
Gent. Coroner at Cockfield on William Norman Jun., who
was killed by falling about 40 feet from a basket in which
he was sitting to repair the walls of the steeple, the rope by
which the basket was suspended having broke. Other persons
had been working in the same basket, and the parties doubt-
less considered it safe; but it is a most dangerous practice to
trust to a single rope at so great a height. Verdict, accidental
death.')*

Towers and Steeples

*This is one of a number of cases where expressions used
by William Scarfe appear to have a slightly different
meaning today. Cockfield Church does not have, nor did
it have, a 'steeple'. William Scarfe clearly means the church
tower. Thomas King, another nineteenth-century Suffolk
diarist, quoted later, also applies the word 'steeple' to
churches on the Norfolk-Suffolk border suffering damage
to their towers in violent storms – see the entry for July
1834. Unfortunately, a climb to the top of Cockfield
church tower failed to reveal young Norman's initials,
although others have carved their initials there.*

1827 Apr 26   Mrs Payne Died was Bured at Bayton Near Bury
She Lived at Cockfield Green Near Felsham

(Elizabeth Payne, aged 49, was buried at Beyton.)

Cockfield church tower where 'young Norman' fell to his death in 1827

1827 Aug 19   Augest 19 1827 will Ranson of Thorpe was
Taken and Died Sudenly

(William Ranson, aged 60, was buried at Brettenham, 24th August 1827, following a Coroner's Inquest. Unfortunately, newspapers of the time do not seem to have reported it.)

1827 Aug 21   Old Henery Long Died of the Bad Feavours
Got It by going to se his son at Fodingford Near
Glemford

(This probably refers to Henry Long, aged 61, buried at Thorpe 23rd August 1827.)

1827 Oct 6   John Crick of Thorpe was taken in fit Died in
miderley *(immediately)*

(John Crick appears to have been buried, aged 67, at Thorpe, November 11th 1827)

1827   Mrs Last was Bured at Rougham Near Bury St
Edmunds the wife of John Last of Thorpe Green
Farm

(Possibly this refers to Frances Last, aged 53, buried at Rushbrooke 26th August 1827.)

1827   Mrs Lars Died was Bured Risbrook

(It is likely the name should be 'Last' from 'Rushbrooke' and that this is the same person as the one above.)

(At this point, the journal, whilst still recording a large number of deaths, widens its compass to include all manner of events. Though most are quite local, this is not always the case.)

1827 Apr 25   Mr Tommmes Harison Recter of Thorpe Parish
Gave Edward Crick of Thorpe A Grate Coate
Worth 2 pounds Edward Crick labour in the parish

of Thorpe Moriuex that was Soulger *(soldier?)*
(Edward Crick appears in the 1841 Census living close to Folly Farm.)

1827 Apr 26   Mr Mead Genet maddose Street Hanover Squire Derictions to find Jospe Anelling Coach and Horses in London Jospeh Allington Watch man London
Jos Allington Watchman
(William Scarfe appears to have been writing down instructions for an intended journey – see the entry for January 1828. Joseph Allington was William Scarfe senior's brother-in-law. We assume he was a watchman as opposed to a watchmaker. Maddox Street lies just to the south of Hanover Square. The Coach & Horses he mentions may have been the London Stagecoach or more likely, the name of the Coaching Inn it used as a terminus.)

The lure of the city
During the nineteenth century, huge numbers of people left the countryside in search of their fortune. In the 1851 census, only 4,590 people living in Suffolk had been born in London. By way of contrast, over 32,000 Londoners had been born in Suffolk. This movement increased in the second half of the century with the expansion of the railways.

1827 May 6   May 6 1827 Mr Mulley of Thorpe Morriuex sold of his stock and Left his farm

1827 May 10   The Childern from Gedding whent to Stowmarket to be Confarmed by order of Mr Tomes Harison Recter of Thorpe Morrriuex Suffolk

The Felsham Six Bells as it looks today

The Felsham Club *was an early form of local Friendly Society, similar to the Oddfellows and the Foresters. Its purpose appears to have been both social and financial, offering health insurance and a payout on death. The members named came from a number of surrounding villages and were mostly tenant-farmers, small-holders and tradesmen. The club met at the Six Bells at Felsham. Mrs Smith (Parish Clerk for Felsham) has described how, during the first half of the twentieth century, a club known as 'The Jolly Boys' met at the Six Bells. They paid 1s 6d entrance and 1s 6d a month, and if anyone was sick, he received a small sum to tide him over. Each year ended with an evening of entertainment given by the members themselves and any remaining money was shared out. This may have been the last vestige of William Scarfe's Felsham Club. The Suffolk Record Office at Bury St Edmunds has a copy of the Rules and Regulations of the Jolly Boys' Society, dated about 1910.*

1827 May 14   George Treares Entered in to The Club at
              Felsham Beels at Newport Elleys

              *(To our surprise, this was not a mistranscription. Newport
              Ely turned up in the banns for Great Whelnetham. He had
              married his second wife, Elizabeth Crick in May 1795. The
              Ely family were landlords of the Six Bells at Felsham until
              shortly after this time. From 1828, William & Sarah Kinsey
              were named as landlords there.)*

1827 May 24   Brettenham field Whent the Bounds of the town
              Mr Cole Recter

              *(It was common to beat the bounds at this time of year, on or
              around Ascension Day. The rector and officers of the parish
              would walk round the boundaries of the parish and beat the
              local boys with willow wands so that they would remember
              where the boundaries were. The practice was often allied to
              the Rogation Days when the rector would lead his parish-
              ioners around the fields to bless the crops.)*

1827 Dec   George andrs an Edward Jennies and Robrt
              Long Ded steal two Cheeses out of a Cart be
              Longing to Samuel Rush of Thorpe on the Road
              Coming from Bury fair George andres was freed
              and Jennies Robert Long Sent to prison two month
              in prison heard leabour

              (According to the Bury Quarter Session Records for

---

Bury Fair

*Three annual fairs were held at Bury St. Edmunds. On
Easter Tuesday and the two following days, there was a
fair for the selling of cattle. On 2nd October and for
several days afterwards, a fair was held for toys, fancy
articles and for the people's pleasure. The December
fair, held on the first of the month, was the principal fair
and was for the sale of cattle and dairy goods.*

*Epiphany 1828, Robert and John Long were 'severally con-
victed of larcenies and severally are ordered to be imprisoned
in the House of Correction and kept to hard labour for two
months'. This was the new Bury Gaol, built in 1803 to a revolu-
tionary design. It was planned by the gaol's first governor, John
Orridge, who also designed a gaol for the Czar of Russia.)*

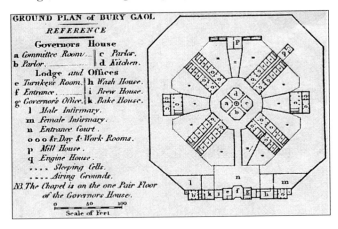

28 Jan 11   Mr Mead Gennet Maddose Street Hanover Squie
Coach and horses In London for Jospeh allington
Watchman
(See the entry for 26th April 1827.)

1828 Jan 11   Mrs Coock was Bured at Felsham she was
Brought from London she was Taken in a fit and
died
*(Elizabeth Cook, aged 49, was buried at Felsham 12th
January 1828.)*

1828 Jan 16   John Scarfe of Hessett Gave his Brother Wm and
his Son 2 pigs worth 18 Shillings a pece

1828 Jan 16   The same night 2 Men Lost Ther Lives being so
Dark one fell in to a Ditch one went into a pound
thay Boath Ware Drowned

(The Suffolk Herald *refers to 'the country now in a very flooded state'. Heavy snow had been followed by a rapid thaw. The newspaper voiced its concern about changing climate and more volatile weather patterns. This entry gives so little detail, it is hard to be sure which stories William Scarfe had heard, or the source of his information. As he did not name the victims, it seems reasonable to suppose they were not local men and the two following newspaper accounts are likely to be the ones he was writing about.)*

The Bury Post *for January 1828 reported that at Sudbury, T. Goldsmith, Coroner for the borough, conducted an inquest on the body of Robert Brighton who was found drowned behind Mr Orbell's water-mill the morning after having spent the evening with several of his friends. It was assumed that in returning home, the unfortunate man had missed his path and fallen into the river. A verdict of 'Found Drowned' was recorded. A week later, this report from Norfolk was published:*

The waters in our river are swollen to such a height, by the vast quantity of rain that has fallen, as well as by the rapid dissolution of the snow which has taken place during the last few days, that a wherry, in attempting to pass through Blackfriars Bridge on Thursday morning, was stopped by the chimney, which was not more than a foot higher than the hatches.

On Thursday last an inquisition was taken by Wm. Lemmon, Gent. Coroner, at the Bridge Inn, Outwell, in this county, on view of the body of Barnabas Turner, aged 35 years, who, returning home from Wisbech the preceding evening, and it being extremely dark, fell into a dike or pool of water in Outwell aforesaid, and was accidentally drowned.—Jurors' verdict accordingly.

1828 Jan 21 Sarah Boggies of Bury was taken and lost the strength of one side

1828 Jan 22 *(George Anders & Edward Jennies & Robert Long – see entry for December 1827)* January 22 1828 tried

1828 Jan 25 George Haward was drawing for a Soulder

(Each parish was required to supply one or two men each year to serve in the Militia, a form of Home Guard. This was not popular, and volunteers were not always forthcoming. The absence of the main wage-earner left families in poverty and accounts of many local parishes of the time list payments to families of men serving in the Suffolk Militia. It was common for the able-bodied men of a parish to be forced to draw lots to determine who would represent them. George Haward seems to have drawn the short straw.)

Avoiding the Militia

The number of men recruited from each village or town reflected the size of the population. Thorpe had to supply one man aged between 18 and 45, of more than five feet two inches in height. Larger parishes like Thurston supplied two men; Rattlesden at this time had to find three. Substitutes could be paid to serve and were often advertised for. It could cost in excess of 40 guineas to buy the services of such a man and agencies were set up for this purpose. You could even insure against your name being drawn by contributing to the Militia Society.

Felsham parish church

1828 Jan 25   Wm North got his amam *(?)* and gave Maria a Gould

(As he writes 'Could' for 'cold', perhaps 'Gould' means something made of 'gold'.)

1828 Jan 28   Mr John Clarke and wife Ann Clements was Marridged at Felsham . . .

(The parish register gives the date of the wedding as 24th January 1828.)

1828 Jan 28   . . . Whent to Barton to Keep the weding at Mr Sadman Felsham wringers Rayzed the Belles for him Atended by Mr Geore Cornell and Miss Kembel Of Thorpe

1828 Jan 30   Mary Scarfe was Taken with a fit of the ager

(She was the wife of William Scarfe senior. Aged 56 at this time, she recovered and lived another 22 years.)

1828 Jan 31 John Mulley of Thorpe Died of the Feavor

(No John Mulley was found buried at this point: Robert Mulley, aged 58, was buried at Thorpe 7th February 1828.)

1828 Feb 10 Wm Scarfe Bought a Silk hanckershief of George Howard of Thorpe

1828 Feb 10 Harot allington is in the familey way by Isaac Purkes of Thorpe he whent to prison and whold not have her

At the Bury Quarter Sessions for Epiphany 1828, Isaac Purkiss was committed on a charge of bastardy and ordered to be discharged. This was not the end of the story: see the entry for 25th February 1828.

1828 Feb 18 Wm Gault of Welnathen Died Bured at Welnathen Feb 22 1828

(He was aged 40, buried at Little Whelnetham.)

1828 Feb 25 on the 25 Harot allington was confined with 2 Boayes

Their names were Joseph & Benjamin. They were baptised at Great Whelnetham on 23rd May 1828. Isaac Purkiss,

---

What's in a name - Allington or Alderton?

Harriet Alderton (or was it Allington?) was the daughter of Robert Alderton, the blacksmith in Little Whelnetham, near the area that is still described as Sicklesmere. Much of the difficulty in tracing people at this time lies in the fact that names change with the person writing them. What William Scarfe calls 'Allington' more commonly appears in parish registers as 'Alderton', but also may be Ollington, Ollerton or even Alderson. Such variations were extremely common.

*Labourer, was listed as the twins' father. Benjamin lived
only twenty weeks and was buried at Great Whelnetham
on 20th July 1828. Harriet died at the age of 26 in
December1829. Where Joseph ended up is a mystery;
he was not mentioned in his grandfather's will in 1849.
Harriet Allington (or Alderton) met a very strange end,
a little over a year later, as the* Suffolk Chronicle *for 12th
December 1829 reported:*

ACCIDENTS AND OFFENCES.

A few days ago, a young woman, named Harriet Alderson, of Sicklesmere, Suffolk, was crossing some pasture
ground on her return from Rougham, when she observed
a furious bull making his way towards her. In great fear
she took rapidly to flight, but unhappily the alarm produced
so powerful an effect on her mind, that she became deli-
rious, and died on Saturday last.

1828 Mar 16   Bought a New wascoate of William Went to
Brettenham Church the first time I put it on with Mary

1828 Mar 19   Mr Robert Taylers House Barn Steable Cow
House Hog Sty and all there Clothes funing tureter
(furniture) all ware Burnt by the maid flinging
sum black ases *(ashes)* in to the Rackyard on a
high wind Day all Burnt *(a)*part in one oure time
the Damage is nearly a Thousilan Pound the
primes *(premises?)* be Longing to Mrs Garnham
of felsham Suffolk

*(Though the farm is not named, it must be what was called
Valley Farm and is now called Grove Farm. According to
the tithe apportionment of 1843, that was the only farm
owned by Mrs Garnham in the parish of Thorpe Morieux.)*

1828   the 19 Mr Taylers house burn and Steabel all
flew on fire all Burn burnt down a midon Tiley
(immediately?) the furntey all Consumed and Lost

– 31 –

the valrating is 7 hunard pound

(See the Suffolk Chronicle*'s report, April 1828.)*

> FIRE.—On the 19th inst., about noon, a fire broke out on the farming premises in the occupation of Mr. Taylor, at Thorpe Morieux, in this county, which in a very short space of time consumed the house, barn, stable, and other buildings, together with every article of furniture, (except a bureau and chest of drawers) about 50 coombs of wheat, 50 of barley, and the crop of seeds. Two horses were got out of the stable just before the roof fell in. The fire was occasioned by another instance of the criminal negligence of servants in throwing out ashes. The violence of the wind, and the buildings being thatched and all adjoining, made the progress of the flames so rapid that no assistance could have been of any avail. The buildings, which were the property of Mrs. Garnham, of Felsham, were insured in the Suffolk Fire-Office, but Taylor, unhappily, had adopted no such precaution.

1828 Mar 26   Mrs Clarke was put to Bed with a fine Gall

(This is a somewhat confusing entry as Susan and John Clarke baptised their son, William at Thorpe on 14th April 1828.)

1828 Mar 28   Mrs Susan Crick the wife of Edward Crick was put to bed with two boayes and a gall about 11 and 12 o clock Thorpe Suffolk the Names of the Childern the firs is Henery the Next is Charles the Next is Sarah

1828 Mar 29   Mr Cole Come to se Mrs Crick and Brought her a Sheet a pair of Blankets and gave her three Shillings

(Mr Cole was the Rector of Brettenham.)

Apr 20   Mrs Harrison whent to Thorpe Church the firs
          Time after she Marrided to Tomes Harrison Rector
          of the Parish

          *(Rev. Thomas Thomas Harrison married Anne Tomlinson on
          2nd October 2nd 1827. According to a parish leaflet of the
          early twentieth century, Anne Harrison brought a sparkle to
          the parish that was missing from her dour husband.)*

Apr 24   Wm Lister and John Puck went to Prison for
          Poching at Mager Harisons maner Brettenham
          *(William Lister lived in an isolated spot, just north-
          west of Folly Farm. The cottage no longer exists.
          He was a bit of a rogue: his name seems synonymous
          with poaching in Thorpe.)*

1828 Apr 28   John North had a fit of the Ager as he was going
              to the Belles *(Felsham Six Bells)* for Beer
              (This means ague, an old word for a fever.)

1828 May   John Hawards wife died May 6 was Burred at
           Thorpe Suffolk

1828 May 20   John Howard wife Died may 20 1828 Was Burred
              at Thorpe by Mr Harrison He married on the 3 of
              november 1828

              *(These last two entries seem to refer to Eliza Howard, aged 28,
              buried at Thorpe Morieux on 19th May 1828. The marriage
              register for Thorpe Morieux records John Haward remarrying
              on 21st October that year. Evidence shows that the vast major-
              ity of men that were widowed remarried, often quite quickly.
              Fewer women remarried if their husbands died young.)*

1828 Jun 4   Edward Crick Children all three Burred tother In
             one grave at Thorpe Church yard
             *(The triplets did not all die at the same time. Charles was
             buried 24th May; Sarah and Henry were buried 4th June.
             The survival rate of multiple birth children was very low.)*

1828 Jun 7   Wm North and Thoms Last Raysed the Roof
of Mrs Garmhams New Barn ocpieds by Robert
Tayler farmer at Thorpe Suffolk

*(See the entry for 19th May 1828 – they seem to have been
rebuilding after the fire. Although the farm is not named, it
was then called Valley Farm and is now named Grove Farm.)*

Maria Marten and the murder in the Red Barn

*There can be few people who have not heard the story of
William Corder and Maria Marten. It has been presented so
many times as the archetypal melodrama: the innocent maid
corrupted, betrayed and finally done away with by the evil
squire. The newspapers, both local and national, were full
of all the lurid details, and the fact the barn at Polstead no
longer exists is in no small
measure a result of 19th-
century trophy hunters
removing the planks as
souvenirs, though eventu-
ally it burned down. The
trial and execution of
William Corder was fol-
lowed eagerly by people
of all classes. Corder*

MURDER.
THE RED BARN, AT POLSTEAD.

*certainly did not 'hang himself by his own confession,' as
William Scarfe asserts. The confession came only hours
before his execution on the morning of Monday 11th August
1831. A crowd of over a thousand, mostly females, flocked
to watch his final drop. Following that, his body was given
to the physicians at Bury Hospital to dissect and conduct
experiments upon. His skin was tanned and used to bind
books, which were in great demand at the time. Pieces of the
rope that dispatched him sold for a guinea an inch.*

1828 Aug 5   Wm Corder was Tried for the muder of maria
martan of Poulsteard a farmers Daughter Theay
found her in the Red Barn be longing to Mrs Corder
Wm Corder Left to be Executed on Monday The 11
of August 1828 he Hung himself by own Confesson
Wm Corder Lived at Poulstard in Suffolk

*(Probably the most famous Suffolk murder. Murder was rare
and this one was particularly shocking)*

28 Aug 7   Esau and Isaac Scarfe of Thorpe was Boarn about
9 oClock in foarnoon in the Parish of Thorpe
Morieux Suffolk Sons of maria Boggies from
Felsham Daughter of J Bogges

Easau and Isaac Scarfe was Boarn that Day that Wm Corder was Tryed

(These are just some of a number of nearly identical entries that appear throughout the book.)

The Confession of William Corder
written in the condemned cell at Bury Gaol, 10th August 1828

I acknowledge being guilty of the death of poor Maria Marten by shooting her with a pistol. The particulars are as follow:-

When we left her father's house we began quarrelling about the burial of the child, – she apprehending that the place wherein it was deposited would be found out. The quarrel continued for about three-quarters of an hour upon this and about other subjects. A scuffle ensued; and during the scuffle, and at the time, I think, that she had hold of me, I took the pistol from the side pocket of my velveteen jacket, and fired. She fell, and died in an instant. I never saw even a struggle. I was overwhelmed with agitation and dismay; – the body fell near the front doors on the floor of the barn. A vast quantity of blood issued from the wound and ran on to the floor, and through the crevices. Having determined to bury the body in the barn (about two hours after she was dead), I went and borrowed the spade of Mrs. Stowe; but, before I went there, I dragged the body from the barn into the chaff-house, and locked up the barn. I returned again to the barn, and began to dig the hole; but the spade being a bad one, and the earth firm and hard, I was obliged to go home for a pickaxe and a better spade, with which I dug the hole, and then buried the body. I think I dragged the body by the handkerchief that was tied round her neck – it was dark when I finished covering up the body. I went the next day and washed the blood from off the barn floor. I declare to Almighty God, I had no sharp instrument about me, and no other wound, but the one made by the pistol, was inflicted by me. I have been guilty of great idleness, and, at times, led a dissolute life; but I hope, through the mercy of God, to be forgiven.

W. CORDER

1828 Oct 15   Mrs Payne was Bured at Bayton she Died at Brettenham

(Anne Payne, aged 64, was buried at Beyton on 14th October.)

1828 Oct 17   Wm Scarfe whent to Bury and Bought A Grate Coat at Mr Hym

(Mr Laurence Hyam, listed as either no. 30 or 31, Buttermarket, Bury St. Edmunds in directories of the time was a tailor and clothes dealer operating from close to where Argos is now)

L. HYAM,
CHEAP NEW HOME-MADE CLOTHES WAREHOUSE,
Wholesale and Retail,
No. 30, BUTTER MARKET, BURY ST. EDMUND'S,

BEGS leave to inform the Inhabitants of Bury and its Vicinity that he has OPENED the above SHOP in the GENERAL CLOTHING LINE, and respectfully solicits their attention to his choice Stock of Ready-made Men's and Boys' Clothes of every description, which he will warrant to be made up at home, of the best materials and workmanship, equal to bespoke; and which he will now offer at such Reduced Prices as not to be excelled by any Shop in the Kingdom.—Plain and Superfine Cloths, Gentlemen's Beaver and Silk Hats, New and Second-hand Watches, with various other Articles, well worth the attention of the Public.

L. H. does not pretend to sell his Goods under prime cost, or without a profit, but his Stock having been recently purchased for Ready Money, in the present depressed state of the market, enables him to offer his Goods for Ready Money at such low Prices that, he flatters himself, will prove highly beneficial to his Customers, and insure him their support and patronage.

Country Shopkeepers supplied Wholesale, with Goods of superior make and quality, below the London Prices. Cloth made up to order of the best materials and workmanship in the first style of Fashion, according to the present scientific method of cutting, at REDUCED PRICES, for READY MONEY ONLY.

N. B. THE LOWEST PRICE AFFIXED AND NO ABATEMENT MADE.

Advertisement from the Bury Post, 1826

1828 Nov 8   Wm Hammonds Wife Died she toke hurt from her daughter was Bured at Watsum meting

(This almost certainly refers to Wattisham Meeting House, but records for this period are incomplete. She appears to have died in childbirth.)

1828 Nov 8   Mrs Hammond She Died at felsham Green the wife of Wm Hammond Melley

(Probably this refers to Elizabeth, née Hunt, who had married William Hammond at Felsham in 1808.)

1828 Dec 10   Mr John Tarbott whent to Mr Andersen tythe feast
Going Hoom fell in to a Ditch and Died found by
G Death

(See the entry for 12th December 1828. By repute, tithe-feasts were lively affairs. There is a superb contemporary account of one such feast in East Anglian Reminiscences *edited by E. A. Goodwyn and J. C. Baxter (Boydell Press, 1976).)*

In all probability, 'going home' meant following a track like this in pitch darkness – not easy with an evening's ale inside you.

1828 Dec 12   John Tayler of felsham Green he Died the Same
Weeke that Mr Talbott at Mrs Dalton of felsham
Mr Talbott was Bured at Stanningfield Near
Cockfield the time Samuel Pesey had a Child Died
of the feavour at Felsham Suffolk

(John Taylor, aged 56, was buried at Felsham 19th December 1828: John Talbott lived at Cockfield Hall. The wife of Samuel Pizzey died around this time – see the entry for 30th July 1829.)

1828 Augst 3 Wm Corder was tried for the murder of maria martain of Polstead a farmers Daughted theay hid in the Red Barn belonging to Mrs Corder Wm Corded left ... to be Executed of augst on monday the 11 1828

G. R.

At the Court at Kensington, *Dec.* 3, 1696,

PRESENT

THE KING'S MOST EXCELLENT MAJESTY IN COUNCIL.

UPON the humble Petition of *Nicholas Brady* and *Nahum Tate*, this Day read at the Board, setting forth, That the Petitioners have, with their utmost care and industry, completed a New Version of the Psalms of David, in English Metre, fitted for public use ; and humbly praying His Majesty's Royal allowance, that the said Version may be used in such Congregations as shall think fit to receive it :

His Majesty, taking the same into his Royal Consideration, is pleased to order in Council, That the said New Version of the Psalms, in English Metre, be, and the same is hereby allowed and permitted to be used in all Churches, Chapels, and Congregations, as shall think fit to receive the same.

W. BRIDGEMAN.

he Hung himself by own Confession In Suffolk Wm Corder lived at Polstead

May 23, 1698.

HIS Majesty having allowed and permitted the use of a New Version of the Psalms of David, by Dr. BRADY and Mr. TATE, in all Churches, Chapels, and Congregations ; I cannot do less than wish a good success to this Royal Indulgence : for I find it a work done with so much judgement and ingenuity, that I am persuaded it may take off that unhappy objection, which has hitherto lain against the Singing Psalms ; and dispose that part of Divine Service to much more Devotion. And I do heartily recommend the use of this Version to all my Brethren within my Diocese.

H. LONDON.

1833 June 12 Jacob Scarfe was Born

1828 August the 9 Esau and Isaac Scarfe of Thorpe was Born about 9 oclock in foarnoon in the Parish of Thorpe morieux Suffolk Sons of maria Boggies from Fyelsham Daughter of J Boggis

1831 April 27 Wm Scarfe B ...

1828 Dec 13   John Scarfe of Hessett Gave Wm a come of wheate the Same Week as Mr Decars was Kill coming from Bury

(Possibly he means 1829. John Parkenson Decarle, aged 56, was buried at St Mary's, Bury St Edmunds, on 15th December 1829.)

The unfortunate death of John Parkerson De Carle

The Suffolk Herald of the time, using yet another spelling of his name, reports the inquisition on the death of this unfortunate man who was killed returning from Bury market.

'It appeared in evidence that a heap of manure had been placed by the side of the road, near the second milestone from Bury (where the road branches off) covered over with road stuff and smoothed so as not to be distinguishable from the road in a dark or dull night: that the deceased left Bury in his gig about 11 o'clock, and that one of the wheels of the gig had passed upon the heap of manure and that the gig had then been drawn forward on one wheel, and the deceased thrown upon his face into the road, where he was found dead.'

The jury, returning a verdict of accidental death, was of the opinion that the heap of manure was **'improperly placed too near the highway'** *and Mr De Carle's demise was* **'occasioned by that obstruction'.**

1828   Wm Parmer was Taken up for a Barsted Child of Hannah Snell of Rougham Near Bury Thomas Spark was Bound for him

(This is a rather confusing entry. Hannah Snell of Rougham was the wife of William Snell, and had married as Hannah Wilkinson the year before. They did not baptise a child until

*1833. A more likely candidate is Lucy Snell who baptised a
bastard child, Louisa, at Rougham on 15th June 1828 and
another named Sophia in 1831. William Palmer was indicted
for larceny in 1830 at the age of 20. He was discharged for
lack of evidence.)*

1829 Jan 25   George Haward and Frances Boggies of felsham
               Ware Published at Thorpe Church

1829 Feb 21   George Haward married to fanney Boggies of
               felsham febwary at Thorpe Church Bixby Goold
               the Clark

Poles stacked after coppicing at Bradfield Wood

febwary the 27 1829 begun Magers Harrisons wood In felsham
               Suffolk

1829 Mar 11   Mrs Scarfe the wife of Mr John Scarfe of Hessett
               Died March 11 1829
               *(Listed in Beyton burial register as Mary Scarpe, aged 74
               – she was nine years older than her husband.)*

– 41 –

1829 Mar 16   *(Mrs Scarfe, wife of John Scarfe of Hesset)* Bured at Bayton the 16 Day of March at half past Two oclock and *(John Scarfe)* ded Give his Brother Wm a Come of Barley

There are several references to John Scarfe giving his brother William quantities of wheat and barley. Possibly this gift was part of the funeral ritual.

1829 Mar 18   Mr Robert Tayler of Thorpe Hiard Rices Hall at Brettenham be Longing to Marger *(Major)* Harrison of Copford Hall ocpied by Mr Harper of Hitcham Hall Suffolk Lived in Mrs Garnham farm at Thorpe Moriuex 1829 oct 11

(This was the same unfortunate man whose belongings were lost when Mrs. Garnham's farmhouse was burnt down – see the entry for 19th March 1828. Though the farm appears to have been rebuilt with the insurance money, Robert Taylor clearly felt it was time to move on. Ryece Hall, Brettenham, is very close by. Since 1948, the Buckmaster family has owned Ryece Hall. They also own and manage Great Hastings Wood, one of the areas of woodland formerly worked by William Scarfe.)

Ryece Hall, Brettenham

1829 Mar 18   Miss Harrison Call at our Hous and Gave the young Child a Shilling wone of the Twins Esau the ouldest

1829 Mar 19   Mager Harrison wanted wm Scarfe and his wife to go to Live at Brook Hall I Could not go

(Brook Hall, Felsham was then occupied by Edward Clements and subsequently by Samuel Melton instead. We have no indication why William Scarfe could not go. Possibly he preferred to ply his trade as a woodman rather than serve as another man's Steward. This is one of very few entries written in the first person.)

1829 Mar 19   four Men carred to prison the same Day for selling of wood

With so little detail, we cannot be sure, but the case may be the one recounted by the Suffolk Herald *for 25th March 1829: Alfred Powle, William Wyard, James Cousens and Webb Taylor were that day convicted of 'trespassing upon the premises of John Loake Esq. of Hadleigh and cutting down several young trees and also lopping some pollard trees, his property, and refusing to pay the penalty.' Powle*

Brook Hall, Felsham

and Wyard received a prison sentence of six weeks, Cousens and Taylor were gaoled for one month.

1829 Mar *(?)*   Henery Goold of Brettenham had a sale for the Benfet of his crederes *(creditors?)*
(He was a blacksmith.)

1829 Apr 16   Mrs Dalton of felsham Died Bured at Bury St Edm
(Sarah Dalton, no age listed, was buried at St Mary's, Bury St Edmunds, on 23rd April 1829.)

1829 May 10   Bought Two Pigs £1 of George andres *(George Andrews)* of Thorpe Samuel How Bought 2 Pigs Same Time of G Andres

1829 Jun 9   Mrs Crick Confined with a Gall Mrs Scarff put her to Bed
(The daughter's name was Sarah. The word 'felsham' is added which may explain the different spelling of 'Scarff' it was another Mrs Scarff from Felsham.)

1829 Jun 10   George Howard fell of the waggon coming from Stowmarket
(He appears later in January 1830 selling beer from his house. Possibly this had something to do with his falling off the cart.)

1829 Jun 21   George Howard came home from Stowmarket workehouse from being heart by the waggon bought by James Boggis of Felsham.
(The workhouse has for many years been known as Stow Lodge and is now converted into flats.)

1829 Jun   In June George Cornell Could not pay for his

Cloathes Mr Sarman Tayler of Rattelsden
(Abraham Salmon, tailor)

1829 Jul 1   Thos Brurds Daughter Died in the New Horspital
Bury St Edmunds Brought to felsham to be Bured
(Susannah Brewer, aged 21, was buried at Felsham on 5th July 1829.)

1829 Jul 1   John Tweed Bate the felsham Club by Taken in
Mr John Goold James Boggies S overaged George
Faires Stward

1829 Jul 2   Hannah Borley *(aged 66)* the wife of Samuel
Borley of felsham Died and was Bured with Susan
Brewed both Bured on the Sunday July 5 by Thos
Anderson of felsham
(See the entry for 1st July.)

1829 Jul 4   Thomas Harrison named and crissend his son
(Thomas Haynes Harrison)

Stow Lodge today

1829 Jul 4   Mr Anderson of Felsham whent to dine with Mr Harrison of Thorpe Morriuex

(This was, in all probability, a very grand affair, judging by reports of the way they both lived.)

To live like a Rector

Suffolk's rectors lived exceptionally well. With many living on incomes of from five hundred to a thousand pounds per annum, they could entertain lavishly, employing a number of servants. In a letter from Reverend Thomas Anderson's sister to Mrs Tilney, written some years later, we read: 'Mr. Anderson, being well off, made his house very comfortable . . . there were 2 feather beds to every bedstead. He also kept what used to be called a very good table.' She then goes on to draw a plan of the table as arranged for a dinner party:-

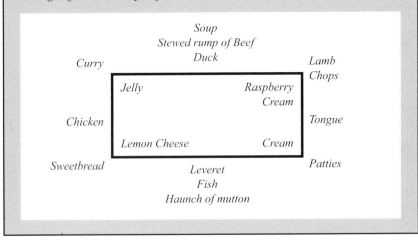

Soup
Stewed rump of Beef
Duck

Curry   Lamb Chops

Jelly   Raspberry Cream

Chicken   Tongue

Lemon Cheese   Cream

Sweetbread   Patties

Leveret
Fish
Haunch of mutton

1829 Jul 17   begun the flower Bought of Mr faonley *(Farnley)* of felsham

1829 Jul 18   the 18th Day a Sharpe Tempest came over Heare

(The Suffolk Chronicle *for 25th July 1829 describes some of the damage caused across Suffolk by this tempest, including a house being struck by lightning in nearby Hitcham.)*

1829 Jul 24   Mager Harrison and Mr Edward Clements had a Grate quarl *(quarrel)* at Brook Hall concearning the House Keeper

1829 Jul 26   John Wright Jun Was Bured at Gedding Suffo
(aged 38)

1829 Jul 30   Saml Pizey of felsham Marred to Mrs Kinzey maid his wife Died In December 1828 Mrs Kinzey Gave them sum Jen *(gin?)* out the Church Gate
(Samuel Pizzey had married Mary Ann in 1816; his second wife, the maid, was Catherine Melton. By this date William and Sarah Kinsey were the publicans at Felsham Six Bells, which is directly opposite the church gate.)

Felsham church gate

1829   very Wett four part of the Harvest It Rayned for severel Days aBot felsham fair Time
(In a contemporary diary, Thomas King, a miller at Thelnetham, describes this as being an appallingly wet harvest; see the entry for 10th January 1830 for more details of this other diary.)

FELSHAM FAIR.

WILLIAM DARBY

BEGS to inform his Friends and the Public, that his DANCING BOOTH will be at FELSHAM FAIR, on the 16th and 17th inst., and conducted with its usual regularity.

COMIC SINGING will be introduced between the Dances.—Tea, &c. will be provided.

An advert from the Bury Post *of the time.*

1829 Aug 16   Mr *(J)*ohn Scarfe was come to Felsham fair the 16 Augest

(A lamb fair was held annually at Felsham on 16th August. Felsham was granted the right to stage markets and fairs as early as 1290. What came to be known as 'The Felsham Peddling Fair' was abolished in 1872 following complaints about drunkenness and vandalism.)

1829 Aug 18   Maria Scarfe Whent to Felsham fair She had not Been Theare for more then a yeare thay carrided the two twines *(Esau and Isaac, William's twin grandsons)*

1829 Aug 20   George Howard Littel Child Died Burred 23 Thorpe

(This was Henry Howard, aged 3 months. In Moyses Hall Museum, Bury St Edmunds, is a child's bier from Thorpe Morieux church, though it appears to be from a slightly later period than this.)

1829 Sep 14   young Cartar of Rattelsden fell Down and a tumbrel Loded with stone wen over him and he Died

(This was Henry Carter who, aged 22, was buried at Rattlesden on 17th September 1829. One can but surmise why so many people in this journal died in accidents involving carts. Possibly the strength of the local beer had something to do with it.)

1829 Sep 14   Mr William North was taken Bleeding at the mouth for tow Houres He have Ben Ill for a Time Died on the 19 Day about 7 o clock in moring of Septem was Ill for half a year

(Aged 52, he was buried on 24th September at Thorpe. Tuberculosis was a major killer at the time and would be a likely diagnosis. Death certificates listing causes of death were not introduced until 1837.)

1829 Oct 11   abraham Sutton whent to Live at Drinkstone Mudds house

1829 Oct 17   toke ann Makings to Keep Daughter of ann Makings from Cockfield Lived at Mr Bucks at Nowton Hall near Bury St Edmunds Suffolk

1829 Oct 18   Sarah Crick was Boarn on WhiteSunday 1829 was Recived in the Church Octo 18 Daughter of Edward and Susan Crick of Thorpe Suffolk Labour

Passengers going to Bury Fair (from an engraving of 1770)

1829 Oct 21   Joseph aves when to Bury faire got Hurt and hisDaughter by a Horse Running Away in the faire Left his Daughter at Mrs Elles Sougate Street Bury St Edmunds

(The Ellis family of 75, Southgate Street were wheelwrights.)

1829 Nov 16   begun Mager Harison felsham wood

(Felsham Wood belonged to the Harrisons: Thorpe and Hastings Woods were owned by the Sparrow family of Gosfield Park, Essex.)

William Scarfe, the Woodman

We know from tithe return of 1843 that William Scarfe and his son were working the woods known as Thorpe Wood, Felsham Wood and Hastings Wood. Though no trees are ever mentioned by name, we can tell from the activities he describes that he was harvesting oak, ash and hazel. The latter two would have been coppiced on a 7–12 year cycle. Today, Bradfield Wood, only a few miles away, is still coppiced in the old way. Formerly known as Felsham Hall Wood, this ancient woodland appears in a number of standard works as a model for systematic replenishable felling. Oliver Rackham's Ancient Woodland: Its History, Vegetation and Uuses in England *describes how woodland in this area was managed.*

1829 Nov 20   Mr John Stearns Mother Died at Thorpe aged 82 bured at Thorpe Moriuex Suffolk

(Hannah Stearn – in the burial register, she is aged 87.)

Mr Harrison made a Sarmon for Her the 9 Chapter of Hebrews 27 verse Theare is apointed for a man onc to Dyed

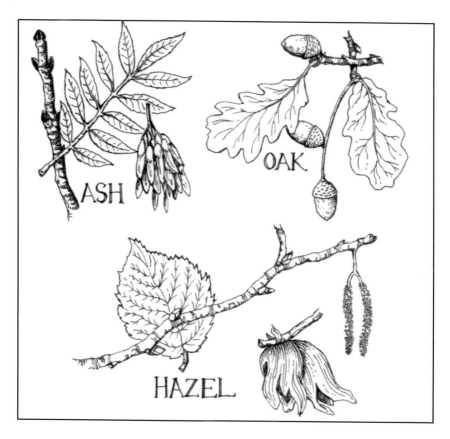

1829   November the weather begun to be vey could whe could not Half work till feb 1830 for 11 weeks or more Wm Scarfe and his son

1829 Nov 25   begun to Snow Lasted Till Jan 31 1830 Thorpe

1829 Nov 25   a Deep snow fell thew *(thawed)* on the 26

1829 Nov 25   a Deepe snow fell in Nov 25 1829 Larsted til feb 1830 The Snow was very Deep the Rods was Block up

1829 Nov   In the mont of november some Roges *(rogues)*
Brook In to a Jenttillman *(gentleman's)* House at
South Harsted and Killed 7 Pursons and Robbed
the hous

*(This is the most intriguing and the most irritating entry
in the whole book. Murder was rare and multiple murder
almost unknown. Newspapers of the time have yielded
nothing. Where is South Harsted? No such place exists. The
year may be wrong. Though the entry appears on a page
with other entries dated 1829, this one may be different.
Nevertheless, it is surprising that such a dramatic account
has failed to offer enough evidence to track this story down.
This cannot be a Suffolk story. The source may be a murder
ballad, such as were sold at the time, recounting – in rather
bad verse – particularly gory murders.)*

1829 Nov 29   John Milton was Crissned at Thorpe Church 20
years of age by T Harrison Rector of Thorpe

1829 Dec 11   Wm Scarfe Toke Thorpe wood to cart of Mr
Jossylen of Sprotong Stward for Mr Sparrow of
Gorsfield near Glemsford

*(White's Directory of 1844 lists J. Josselyn as a landowner
in Sproughton near Ipswich. James Goodeve Sparrow was
Lord of the Manor and a principal landowner. He resided at
Gosfield Park in Essex. Mr Josselyn was his Steward at this
time and resided at Thorpe Hall.)*

The Sparrow Family

*In the Oakes Diaries, edited by Jane Fiske, James Oakes, a
rich merchant in Bury writes in 1826 of his dealings with
James Goodeve Sparrow. Sparrow was a partner in the
Suffolk & Essex Bank (Crowe, Sparrow, Brown & Co.),
Buttermarket, Bury St Edmunds. Sparrow died in 1838
and was succeeded by his son Henry.*

> **A comb of wheat**
>
> *This was just one of many such gifts noted in the book. William was the recipient of a good deal of help from his elder brother. Details such as this appear throughout the journal. A comb or coomb of wheat was four bushels. A bushel was something in excess of a cubic foot in volume. Woodmen were notoriously poor. William Scarfe's survival owed much to his brother's generosity.*

1829 Dec 12   John Scarfe of Hessett gave his Brother Wm a come of Tail Whate

1829 Dec 23   Mary Baldwine of Thorpe Died *(aged 47)* Bured on the 27 the Sunday after Cristmiss Day1829 Wm North Made The Coffeen for Mary Balwine of Thorpe Moriuex Suffolk Died of a soar in Her Thorte after a Long She Have Ben Ill for A Time
(William North lived at the cottage now called 'Wheelwrights' and was a carpenter and wheelwright. His workshops were across the other side of the road, opposite the cottage.)

1829   Wm Scarfe and his wife whent to the Buron *(?)* From Thorpe Morriuex Suffolk 1829
(This may mean Great Barton. Four years later, William's brother was to buy him his house from Pearson Sharman, a miller of Great Barton, near Bury St Edmunds. Alternatively, and more likely, it may refer to the manor court which was sometimes called the Baron Court. See the entry for 11th July 1840 for details of the manor court.)

1829   Mager Harrison of Copford Hall Essex 1829

The home of William North, wheelwright.

1830	for the year of 1830 The Psalms of David to be Red Every Day in the week

1830   In 1830 the winter was very Had The farmers
        Bought Some coale for the poor in Every Town
        (The Suffolk Herald *for December 1829 reported that 'the
        Royal Edmund Lodge of Freemasons, with that benevolence
        that has always characterised their body generously voted
        ten pounds from their funds to assist in furnishing the poor
        of the town in coals during this inclement season'. The
        Lodge was reported as being 'rather surprised that no
        general subscription has yet been set on foot in the town
        for this purpose'; and they trusted that 'the noble example
        of the Edmund Lodge' would be 'promptly and effectually
        followed'.)*

1830 Jan 1   George Howard of Thorpe begun to Sell Best Beer
              and Tabel Beer

(This was the man who had fallen off the wagon coming back from Stowmarket in June the previous year. Like William Scarfe Junior, he was married to a Boggis of Felsham.)

1830 Jan 1   Frank How of Felsham married on New years Day to Myme Bixby Daughter of Jeremier Bixby of felsham

(Francis Howe and Jemima Bixby)

1830 Jan 1   Robert Pilbrow the younger strick a man with A moul spade on the Head and he Died from the Blow Pilbrow went to prison to Stand Trial

(Pilbrow's name does not appear in the lists for the Quarter Sessions and he is not reported as coming to trial at the County Assizes. He did not hang; nor was he transported. We can only assume it was regarded as self-defence and he was discharged. The prison registers for this time no longer survive.)

1830 Jan 3   Mrs Scarff whent to se Mrs Bird stayed a good

The Three Grades of Beer
By this time, beer had largely replaced ale as the drink of the masses. Best Beer was produced from the first brewing and was superior in flavour and alcohol content. Table beer was more of an everyday drink. There was also small beer, which was described as the daily intake of the working classes and servants. This was weak and cheap, but probably safer than the drinking water, and even children drank it. Following the Licensing Act of 1828, a new Beer Act allowed almost any householder to sell beer, providing he held an excise permit. Magistrates frequently commented about an increase in criminal behaviour as a result of this piece of legislation.

wile and Henery Grimwood of Thorpe Thay Boath
Have Ben Ill for Some Time

1830 Jan 10 January 10 and 11 a Deep Snow fell snew for 2
Days at times whe could not work in Thorpe wood
Lorst 3 weekes Wm Scarfe of Thorpe Morruex
Suffolk

*(Thomas King of Thelnetham in his diary describes the
weather for January 1830 as 'very sharp rime frosts with
plenty of snow'. The newspapers of the time mention a
number of deaths from skaters falling through thin ice. There
were also problems of flooding and swollen rivers at fording
points when the thaw came.)*

1830 Jan 10 a Deep Snow fell it Snew for 5 Day begun to thow
the 5 night the snow was very Deep at Pleaces the
popel had to thow the Snow in the Rod

1830 Jan 10	10 11 12 13 a Deep snow fell It snew Hard Eevery Day whe could not Do aney wrok Lorst 3 Day

1830 Jan 10   10 11 12 13 a Deep snow fell It snew Hard Eevery
               Day whe could not Do aney wrok Lorst 3 Day

1830 Jan 15   Sarah Goold Died the Mother of Joseph Goold of
               Thorpe 86 years age
               (See the entry for 21st January 1830.)

1830 Jan 15   Mrs Green from Sutton Hall was bured at Comes
               Near Stowmarkett
               (Margaret Darby Green, aged 87, was buried at Combs.)

1830 Jan 15   Mr Kizenys *(Mr Kinsey's)* Ball was the same night
               Mr Walton of Bradfield Lay was the Hed at Mr
               Kinzey Ball at felsham Bells In Suffolk
               *(Thomas Walton is listed in White's Directory of 1844 as
               living at Bradfield Lodge in Bradfield St Clare.)*

1830 Jan 15   our Two Little Twines had the water pock thay
               both ware very Ill for a Day Thay could not Rest
               for a Night
               *(According to an early edition of Webster's Dictionary, this
               was chicken-pox.)*

1830 Jan 15   Thos andres was Taken very Bad Have ben Ill for
               Some Time He is not Like to Recover Wm Scarfe
               When to se him on the 16 day And found Him
               very Bad Staided with Him som Time His sons
               And Daughters was Theare To se Him at Thorpe
               (See the continuing story on pages 58 and 60.)

1830 Jan 16   John Garrad Miller at preston His Boy Tok some
               Bread of His Name He said the Boy Should go to
               prison for Doing the Crime

1830 Jan 16   *(Thomas Andrews)* Recived from the felsham Club

£	s	d
3	13	0
5	15	
9	8	0

8 week at 9 shillings per week

1830 Jan 18   Thos Andres of Thorpe Died the felsham Club 43 persons attended Him to the Burel at Thorpe

(Thomas Andrews, aged 56)

The safety net of The Felsham Club

Before National Insurance, Friendly Societies provided money in times of need. Of course, you had to be able to afford the weekly subscriptions. It appears that William Scarfe did not need to 'call on the club' until 1843 when his health was failing. What William Scarfe calls 'The Felsham Club' may have had another name. It has not been possible to trace any details beyond what William Scarfe writes. However, it should not be confused with the West Suffolk Friendly Society which was founded in 1830. The Felsham Club was well established by then.

1830 Jan 21   Josp Gould of Thorpe Bured His Mother at Felsham Ded at Thorpe

(Sarah Gould, aged 86)

1830 Jan 21   old Mrs Garnern Died In felsham Parish House once was A farmer at Felsham Suffolk

(Mary Gardiner, aged 59, was buried on 25th January. Parish houses for the sick and elderly continued to be maintained in many villages long after the establishment of Union Workhouses.)

The Benefit Clubs and Friendly Societies of Suffolk

These began to emerge at the end of the eighteenth century in order to 'encourage self-reliance and mutual self-help among working men.' These were the words of John Glyde reporting later in the nineteenth century on the 489 Benefit clubs that were known to have existed in 1872, serving over 23,000 members in Suffolk. 'The system,' he asserted, 'tempts a man to save out of the earnings of health and strength for the needs of sickness and age.' However, these groups were not always successful. In 1872, 300 groups failed to publish returns, many having gone under through lack of funds in time of hardship or epidemic. Though little remains as evidence for the Felsham Club, it appears to have been economically sound and had a fair number of members in a dozen or more parishes. It drew its membership largely from tenant farmers and craftsmen such as wheelwrights, carpenters and shoemakers.

Benefit Clubs were of three kinds...
1. Affiliated societies or orders such as the Odd Fellows or the Foresters.
2. County or patronised societies such as the West Suffolk Friendly Society and the Stowmarket Provident Society. In 1853, Needham Market Friendly Society collected just over £278 in fees from its members and paid out over £470 on sickness and death. The society could only cope with this shortfall as it had over £2,500 on account, earning interest.
3. Local town and village societies, often attached to and meeting at the local public house. These were the most vulnerable, often having little in reserve when times were hard. However, the Felsham Club seems to have thrived, as did other local societies such as the 'United Friendly Society' of Rattlesden. It is known that a leading light in this movement was Professor Henslow, Rector of Hitcham, mentioned later in this book as a pioneer of the Allotment scheme. He established a benefit club in Hitcham along the lines of the highly successful scheme already in operation in Long Melford.

1830 Jan 22   Fredrick Mudd of Gedding Died *(aged 46)* Brother
to the Docter Frank Mudd

1830 Jan 24   Thos Andres of Thorpe was Bured by Mr Dasely
of Lavenham he made a Good sermon count of
his Burell at Thorpe Moriuex Suffolk 44 porsons
Atended Him

1830 Jan 24   Thos Andres was Bured at Thorpe

corst for his funel	11	5	1
Toke oute for Beer and vitles one shilling a Man	2	12	0
Mr Poulters Bill for Hats binds and Gloves ribbens and chees	2	6	7
Wm Scarfe for go after popel		2	6
(total)	5	1	1

1830 Jan 25   Henery Grimwood of Thorpe was very Ill had a
Bad foot for sometime

1830 Jan 27   Fredrick Mudd was Bured at Gedding near
felsham

1830 Feb 2   and *(snow)* Larsted for 11 or 12 weeks whe Lost a
Grate Deal of Time Feb 2 1830
(See the entries for 10th, 11th, 12th and 13th Jan 1830.)

1830 Feb 6   Mrs Morgan Died at Felsham wife of Benjiman
Morgan Late of Gedding Lars
*(Elizabeth Morgan, aged 78, was buried at Gedding on 12th
February 1830.)*

1830 Feb 8   very Grate flood after the Thaw the snow
wasted a grate peace

(This was widespread after such a depth of snow rapidly thawed. One story in the Suffolk Chronicle *of the time describes how a butcher at Finningham lost a load of meat because he tried to take a horse and cart across a swollen ford.)*

1830 Feb 8   Mr Charles Coock marrided to Miss Sarah Tayler of felsham farmer

(Charles Cook married Sarah Taylor at Felsham.)

1830 Feb 13   Frank How sed he wold joine the felsham Club

(Francis Howe was the blacksmith at Felsham.)

1830 Feb 14   Mr Croker from Lavenham Preashed at Thorpe Church

1830 Feb 14   Frank How Entred into the felsham Club And is Clark for the Club

1830 Feb 15   Mrs Clark whent to Mr Grouses for old Mrs Gault of Bilerston and careard a bottel of her water

(Mr Robert Growse, of Duke St, Bildeston, was listed in White's directory for 1844 as a surgeon. His two sons became surgeons in Bildeston after him. Robert's elder brother, John Growse, was surgeon in Hadleigh. He too had a son who became a doctor.)

1830 Feb 15   Josp aves whent to Bury and Sould his Hobby

1830 Feb 23   Josp Aves Sould his Hobby for 12   0   0 and bought *(a)*nother

(A hobby is an archaic word for a small horse. Joseph Aves was a shoemaker.)

1830 Feb   in the month of feb John Birds wife of Thorpe was very Ill for Some Time

(See the entry for 17th April.)

The house of Mr Growse the surgeon at Bildeston

1830 Feb   John Treasy from Bretenham was Cut in the new
            Horsptill at Bury and was cureard He was Cut for
            the Gravell by Doctor Dalton at Bury

*(John Tracey was probably operated on for kidney or blad-
der stones. Samuel Pepys, over 150 years earlier, survived
such an operation. 'Cut for the gravel' was an expression
used at the time and was regarded in awe by country folk.
People who survived such operations became minor local
celebrities. John Tracey died at Brettenham almost exactly
a year later, aged 50. Dr John Dalton served as a surgeon
at Suffolk General Hospital between 1825 and 1843; he is
known to have assisted at the dissection of William Corder's
body – see the entry for August 1828.)*

1830 Mar 19   Martha Vince Died of Thorpe Moriuex Suffolk
               (Aged 63, she was buried at Thorpe on 24th March.)

> ## The 'New' Bury Hospital
> The Suffolk General Hospital, which opened in 1826 near the bottom of Westgate Street in Bury St Edmunds, was designed to treat as many as 50 in-patients at a time, as well as dealing with a number of out-patients. It was built as a result of public subscription and wards such as the fever ward were later added through private benefaction. The building which housed part of the hospital had formerly been a Military Depot.

The Bury Hospital

1830 Mar 20   Wm Scarfe Hurt his Thoat at Bury

1830 Mar 20   Benjamin Smith wife Died his daughter died in 1839

(Mary Ann Smith, aged 37, was buried at Thorpe on 25th March 1830. Elizabeth Smith, aged 16, was buried at Thorpe on 31st March 1839.)

1830 Apr 2 It Snowed at times All the Day long whe Loded a Load of Pooles to go to Stowmarket

(According to Ray Tabor, in his book Traditional Woodland Crafts, *poles were two inches or more in diameter; otherwise, they were known as rods.)*

Coppicing still goes on today at Bradfield Wood and Hastings Wood.

1830 Apr 17 Mr Hammond of felsham Died Bured on the 24 Miller and farmer

(Charles Hammond, aged 80, was buried at Felsham on 24th April 1830.)

1830 Apr 17 The wife of J Bird Died 10 Days after being confined have been Ill Ever since Harvest Lived at the folley farm Thorpe Morriuex Suffolk

(Kerenhappuck Bird was buried at Brettenham, 21st April 1830, aged 30. Thence began a sequence of events – see the entry for October 1831.)

1830 Apr 25 Wm Scarfe whent to Brettenham Meetng the afterNoon.

| 1830 Apr | In the month of April Wm Lister Laid *(?)* Enprison a ganst Saml Clements for Shotting a fephent *(pheasant)* in Hassen *(Hastings)* Wood out of seasen he Ded not pay for the Crime |

(Presumably this is the same William Lister who served time for poaching in April 1828 and whose marital exploits are recounted later. The tithe map shows William Lister as living in what must have been one of the most isolated corners of this part of Suffolk, between Thorpe and Hastings Woods, with no clear road or track to the dwelling.)

Pheasant

1830 May 8   the wife of John Digings of Thorpe was Bured by Mr Harrison Recter of this Parish
(Ann Diggins, aged 70)

1830 May 23   Mr Grimwood wife was Confined with 2 Children boath died
(John & Sarah Ann Grimwade, buried 23rd May at Thorpe.)

1830 May 31   whe all whent to Mr Scarfe of Hessett to Diner MonDay winsentide from Thorpe the Littil Twins theay both when to Hessett

1830 Jun 2   John Ony whent with Mr Grimwoods Waggeon to Tharston for Sand Coming Home fell Down the waggon whent over him and he Died
(We believe this was the man who appears in the Brettenham burial register as John Hoddy (aged 76), buried 13th June

1830. This appears to be borne out by a newspaper article appearing in the Suffolk Chronicle *on 12th June 1830.)*

ACCIDENTS AND OFFENCES.

A shocking accident occurred on Thursday week, in the parish of Hesset, Suffolk, to a poor man upwards of 70 years of age, in the employment of Mr. Eastley, of Thorpe. It appears, that in driving a load of gravel down a hill the horses became unmanageable, and the men endeavouring to stop them, fell, when the wheels passing over him, fractured the leg and thigh most dreadfully. He was conveyed to the Suffolk General Hospital, where he at present lingers in great agony, and we are sorry to add no hope is entertained that his life can be preserved.

1830 Jun 8 Edward Codd of Cockfield married to Ann Euse of felsham Green Brook and sold his goods her father is stward for Mr Thos Anderson of felsham
(This may refer to an Edwin Codd who had married Mary Ann Hewes in 1824 at Felsham.)

1830 Jun 19 John Hunt Thorpe Green Died being a Long time In decline
(This possibly refers to William Hunt, aged 46, buried at Thorpe on 25th June 1830.)

1830 Jun 25 John Scott wife of Felsham Green Died in decline Left Two childeren after Long illneses
(Elizabeth Scott, aged 33, was buried at Felsham on 30th June 1830.)

1830 Jun 26 Wm the 6 come Eare to the crown the old King died June 1830
(It should be William IV – presumably William Scarfe was not too good with Roman numerals.)

1830 Jul 11 George Howards wife was Confined with a Gal Thorpe

(Harriet, born to George and Frances Haward, was baptised at Thorpe on 26th September 1830.)

1830 Jul 28   Mrs Misem Came from Horragnes to felsham
(This is surely Horringer, near Bury St Edmunds. Several people by the name of Mison lived at Horringer at that time.)

1830 Jul 31   July 31 King George Died Burred at Winsor Carsle
(Strangely, there is no such entry for the death of William IV, though there is reference to a feast in June 1838 to celebrate what we know to be Victoria's Coronation.)

1830 Aug 7   ann Makings come to Thorpe for a weekes Haorledy forom Bury St Edmunds and went to felsham faire on the 16

1830 Aug 24   Mr Jacksons farmer of Stoke his House and Barn was set on fire by Sombody
(This seems to herald what was to become a winter marked by riot and disorder. Possibly the farmer was Isaac Jackson who farmed at Brettenham. We were unable to trace a farmer named Jackson at that time in any of the four Stokes in Suffolk.)

1830 Sep 9   King Wm was crowned at London
(Somewhat surprisingly, this is the last royal reference. Queen Victoria fails to get a mention)

1830 Sep 19   Old Mrs Goold the wife of John Goold was Bured at felsham Died with Mr Crouch was Buried by Mr anderson of felsham Mr Wm Pilbrow Clark at felsham
(Amy Gould, aged 100)

1830 Oct 9   Hustler sold of his stock Bacon at felsam

1830 Oct 14   old Mr*(s)* Baldwin of Thorpe Died

(Mary Baldwin aged 86 was buried at Thorpe 26th October.)

1830 Oct   In the month of Octo a man was hurt by the myshene
by the name of Sutton

*(Though we could not find a newspaper entry for this acci-
dent, a number of others we did find were very similar. Such
stories, along with the belief that jobs were being lost to the
new technology stirred up a lot of bad feeling.)*

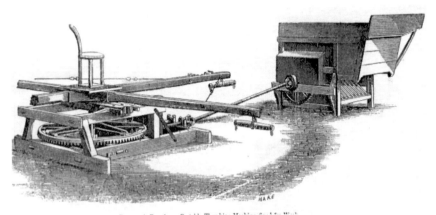

Ransome's four horse portable threshing machine

*The Bury Post for 1st December 1830 reports on a 13 year
old boy named Thomas Andrews who, whilst attending a
threshing machine, 'by some means fell into the hopper, in
which two cylinders revolve . . . the limb was immediately
drawn in, and coming into contact with the beaters, was
mangled in a most shocking manner.' We are informed he
sustained the subsequent amputation with great fortitude.*

1830 Nov 7   Saml Howard John Green of Thorpe fell out

1830 Nov 13   Susan Suel whent to Live with S Borlder She Lift
John Bird of Thorpe Morriuex Suffolk

1830 Nov 13　Susan Snell whent to Live with Saml Baldwin

(This seems to be another version of the previous entry. See also entry for 28th December.)

1830 Nov 15　Robert Snelling Simon Kinzey Robbed Mr Clements Barn of some whate felsham Simon Kinzey owned it to Mr Farnley

(See the entry for 18th November 1830.)

1830 Nov 16　Bought our New Cart Mr Wm North of Thorpe

1830 Nov 18　Robert Snelling was carred to Prison for Robbing Clements Barn at felsham.

(The Bury Quarter Sessions reports for this period record Robert Hunt Snelling, aged 27, convicted of larceny and ordered to be imprisoned in the House of Correction and kept to hard labour for the term of nine months. The Suffolk Chronicle *account includes the information that he stole two coombs of wheat.)*

The gatehouse to Bury Gaol by the late Keith Pilling, reproduced by kind permission of his family

| 1830 Dec 6 | the poor popel ware got together for more wages |
| | *(The 'Swing Riots' had reached Suffolk. The area was known to be a hotbed of discontent. Less than a generation before, in 1816, there had been cases of demonstration and riotous assembly at Gedding, Rattlesden and Wattisham.)* |

| 1830 Dec 10 | Wm Scarfe and his Son was Sworen on Consterble at Bilderston |
| | *(They received three shillings a day as Special Constables, and three shillings for night call-outs. This was in anticipation of the troubles to come. They cannot have been called out many times: the total bill for policing Thorpe Morieux up to Easter was just twelve shillings.)* |

| 1830 Dec 11 | Batley Semmons married to H Cudbert at felsham church by Mr Thos Anderson |
| | *(Battley Seyman married Hannah Cudbard at Felsham on 11th November 1830. She appears in the Overseers accounts* |

A plain statement of the case of the labourers by the Reverend Author

An anonymous letter to the Suffolk Chronicle *on 1st January 1831 said: '. . . The very least and lowest wages a labourer ought to receive for his weekly service is the sum of twelve shillings under the present circumstances of the land. We should be ashamed to hear that the labour of the peasant from dawn to dark has been insufficient to satisfy the hunger of his family, much less to provide them with the decencies and comforts to which every honest man is entitled. Wages of eight shillings or less are common place, only three or four shillings is paid by the parish for work on the roads.' (Those at the time who were able-bodied and residing in parish poor houses were often put to work repairing the roads.)*

for 1829, as she had a bastard child and was being paid for the child's maintenance by Robert Goodwin, the reputed father. The parish accounts record paying Hannah Cudbert the sum of two shillings, weekly: Robert Goodwin payed a yearly sum of £5 4s 0d to recompense the Overseers of the Parish of Felsham. Bastardy was common in the villages and where records survive, in parishes like Cotton and Mendlesham, at least 25% of births were out of wedlock.)

1830 Dec 12   it begun to Snow on the Sunday after i when to Hadligh to pay the Rent for the Thorpe wood

1830 Dec 14   the farmers called a Town Meting for Bennefit of the poor of Thorpe parish

(This may have been more for their own protection. That winter, there were countless indictments for machine-breaking, destroying toll-houses, riotous assembly, conspiring to raise wages, sending threatening letters, arson and extortion.)

1830 Dec 28   Saml Baldwin was marredeged to Susan Snell at Thorpe

(In the parish register, she is listed as Susan Sewell)

1831 Jan 6   Robt Payne And Miss Melten ware married Thorpe Church

(Robert Payne of Brettenham and Mary Ann Melton of Thorpe.)

1831 Jan 6   John Scarfe of Hessett come our Hous gave whe a come of tail whate *(wheat)*

1831 Jan 8   Wm Tayler of Cockfield whent to Bury Goale for Mobbing the New Constables at Cockfield

(William Taylor was one of four from Cockfield convicted of unlawful assembly and bound over to keep the peace.

According to the Suffolk Chronicle *of 8th January 1831,
'William Taylor on the 14th December, with William Olley
assembled tumultuously with many other persons at Cockfield
. . . and were gone in a large body to the house of the rector
of Cockfield.' Under the old poor law, overseers of the parish,
parish constables and leading landowners and clergymen
were largely responsible for the distribution of benefits and
were often the target for such protest. Just before this time,
local newspapers were full of cases of civil   unrest, arson
and the destruction of new machinery. The account opposite is
from the* Suffolk Chronicle *of 16th October 1830.)*

The Swing Riots

*The Swing Riots began in Kent and were a kind of 19th
century peasants' revolt. Low wages, irregular work and
high food prices following bad harvests had spawned unrest
the year before. It reached Suffolk in the winter of 1830/
1831. Inflammatory leaflets, signed under the pseudonym
'Captain Swing,' were read by the more literate members of
the labouring class, and there were gatherings in a number
of local towns and villages. At the Bury Epiphany Sessions
for 1831, John Smith (aged 28), Samuel Smith (29), William
Olley (38) and William Taylor (42), all of Cockfield, were
indicted for riot, rout and unlawful assembly along with
17 others from other villages. They were all found guilty of
unlawful assembly and bound over on surety of £30 apiece to
keep the peace for 12 months. They were the lucky ones. Five
men received gaol sentences of two months. The ringleader,
Joseph Saville (53) was convicted of the misdemeanour of
dispersing inflammatory papers and was given one year's
gaol and a fine of £50. At the same court, seven men were
transported to Australia for breaking the hated new threshing machines that they believed would cost them their jobs.*

OUTRAGES IN KENT.—The county of Kent is in a very agitated state, on account of the organized system of stack-burning and machine-breaking which appears to be established in several extensive districts. The farmers flattered themselves that the large reward which has been offered would have the effect of inducing some of the incendiaries to betray their accomplices, but in this respect they have been hitherto disappointed. On the night of the 5th inst. several corn-stacks in the neighbourhood of Ashe and Lyminge were set fire to and burnt to the ground. One of the sufferers had boasted that, if the incendiaries came to him, he was prepared to meet them with a bushel of bullets. They, however, did come, but his bullets did not save his corn-stacks. It appears that the conspirators do not seek for money or plunder of any kind. On the contrary, when offered money not to destroy property, they have uniformly refused it, and they have on no occasion robbed. We understand that the High Sheriff of the county lately attended one of their meetings in the open air, and addressed them, pointing out to them the folly and wickedness of their proceedings. They appeared to attend to his observations; but previously to dispersing one of them said, "We will destroy the corn-stacks and thrashing-machines this year. Next year we will have a turn with the parsons, and the third we will make war upon the statesmen." What will such a state of things as this end in? It is understood the farmers whose thrashing-machines have been broken do not intend to renew them. So far, therefore, the object of the rioters will be answered. Farmers do not consider thrashing-machines of much advantage, seeing that they throw the labourers out of employment, and consequently upon the parish. Anonymous letters, signed "Swing," have been received by post by two individuals, threatening the destruction of their premises by fire, which has caused great alarm in the families. The dead walls all through the town, and for some miles on the road to Canterbury, bear the same significant word "Swing," written in chalk.

1831 Jan 9   John offord wife was Bured Died in Decline

(Mary Offord, aged 53, was buried that day at Thorpe.)

1831 Jan 12   Mr Raynes of felsham Died Aged 82

(Samuel Rands was buried on 27th January 1831 and appears in the Felsham register as aged 84.)

1831   old Mr Raynes and Mrs Melton fell out concerning the House Keeper Lie with her Master thay whent to Law Mr Raynes Left House Keeper Charlotte Kebbell 2 hundard Pound Felsham Suffolk

(Mrs Melton was Samuel Rands' daughter. She had good cause to be concerned.)

The Will of Samuel Rands

Samuel Rands first wrote a will in 1815 when his wife was still alive. Though she died in 1817, the will allowed for his lands to be sold and the money divided evenly between his daughters, Mary Melton, Amy Taylor and Sarah Sturgeon, 'share and share alike'. In February 1830, he added the first of three codicils to the will, leaving 'Charlotte Keble who now lives with me the sum of thirty pounds'. A second codicil made in July 1830 left Charlotte Keble a further hundred pounds provided she relinquished any rights or interests in any of his lands and properties. In this codicil, Samuel Rands disinherited his daughter Mary Melton.

1831 Jan 23   Mr John Scarfe of Hessett give whe 5 0 0 for our cart . . .

1831 Jan 23   . . . gave whe 5 pound note ones *(owns?)* our New Cart

1831 Jan   in the month of Jan Mary allington whent to prison from Gedding for having a Barsted Child by D edm

(In actual fact, she went before the magistrates to inform them that the father of her child, Ann, was Charles Debenham. A bastardy order issued by the magistrates demanded he should pay twenty-four shillings towards her lying-in, eight shillings for the drawing up of the order and one shilling a week for the child's upkeep.)

The tale of Mary and Ann Alderton/Allington

Following Gedding's insistence on Charles paying for his brief moment of pleasure, Mary next appears in the parish records as Mary Alderton, marrying a widower by the name of William Dedman. This was almost certainly the father of Charles, her former lover. He did have a son called William and it might suggest Mary married the brother of her child's father, but this William Dedman had married in Gedding church earlier that year. Though there were several children named Dedman from this union, the love-child, Ann, continued to be called Ann Alderton. At the age of twenty, in 1851, when working as a servant for Frederick Raker, Ann became pregnant and had a child baptised as Herbert Edward Alderton. Within two months, both mother and child were dead. The survival rate of bastard children was very low. For their mothers, it was not a lot better.

1831 Feb 1   It Snowed very Hard And Wind Blew Hard

1831 Feb 1   grate Deal of snow fell It was very could

1831 Feb 5   Whe Loded a Load of hurdles out of felsham wood the snow was very deep Whe was fost *(forced)* to carry them on our shoulders in to the Rod

1831 Feb 14   Wm Lambert *(aged 66)* Died at Bradfield St Cleare felsham Club attended his funel he was Ill for 1

(No. 31.)

R. B.

The Order of *John Benjafield Esquire and Robert Bevan Esquire* Two of his Majesty's Justices of the Peace in and for the said *County of Suffolk* one whereof is of the Quorum, and both residing next unto the Limits of the Parish Church within the Parish of *Gedding* in the said *County* made the *fifth* Day of *January* one thousand eight hundred and thirty-one concerning a *female* Bastard Child, lately born in the *Parish* aforesaid, of the Body of *Mary Allington* single Woman.

WHEREAS it hath appeared unto us, the said Justices, as well upon the complaint of the Church-Wardens and Overseers of the Poor of the said *Parish* as upon the oath of the said *Mary Allington* that she, the said *Mary Allington* on the *twenty second* day of *November* now last past, was delivered of a *female* Bastard Child, at *the house of Garrish Hole* in the said *County Parish of Gedding* in the said *County* and that the said *female* Bastard Child is *likely to be* chargeable to the said *Parish* of *the said Parish* : and further, that *Charles Debenham* did beget the said Bastard Child on the Body of her, the said *Mary Allington* and whereas *the said Charles Debenham being now personally present before us and having heard the said charge exhibited upon oath in his presence and admits the truth thereof* We, therefore, upon Examination of the Cause and Circumstance of the Premises, as well upon the Oath of the said *Mary Allington* as otherwise, do hereby adjudge him, the said *Charles Debenham* to be the reputed Father of the said Bastard Child. *and further that the said bastard child was born* And thereupon we do Order, as well for the better Relief of the said *Parish* as for the Sustentation and Relief of the said Bastard Child, that the said *Charles Debenham* shall and do forthwith, upon notice of this our Order, pay, or cause to be paid, to the said Church-Wardens and Overseers of the Poor of the said *parish* or to some or one of them, the sum of *twenty four shillings* for and towards the lying-in of said *Mary Allington* and the Maintenance of the said Bastard Child, to the time of making this our Order. *and the* And we do also hereby further order, that the said *Charles Debenham* shall likewise pay, or cause to be paid, to the Church-Wardens and Overseers of the Poor of the said *parish* for the time being, or to some or one of them, the Sum of *one shilling* Weekly, and every week from the present time, for and towards the Keeping, Sustentation, and Maintenance of the said Bastard Child, for and during so long a time as the said Bastard Child shall be chargeable to the said *Parish* And we do further Order, that the said *Mary Allington* shall also pay, or cause to be paid, to the said Church-Wardens and Overseers of the Poor of the said *parish* for the time being, or to some or one of them, the Sum of *one shilling* Weekly, and every Week, so long as the said Bastard Child shall be chargeable to the said *parish* in case she shall not nurse and take care of the said Child herself. Given under our Hands and Seals the Day and Year first above written.

Sum of eight shillings for one order

———◦○◦◀▣▶◦○◦———

T. C. NEWBY, PRINTER, BURY.

The bastardy order for Mary Allington – see the entry for 1st January 1831.

yeare 39 persons atended hem to the Grave he had 50 0 0 from the Club

1831 Feb 14   The ould Milita Was Corled up to Im borded *(embodied)* at Bury St Edmunds.
(See the entry for 25th January 1828.)

1831 Feb 20   Bought two pigs of Gorge Howard for 0 12 0

1831 Feb   it was very Wett whe not carted cart the wood for wett the Rod was very Bad Wm Scarfe Edw Crick John Bird John Long Elfred Goold

1831 Mar 13   Wm Scarfe whent to Cockfield to osborns

The things William Scarfe failed to mention
Most of his entries are about very local matters, as might be expected. However, searching the information of the time, one has to be surprised at what he leaves out. In March 1831, the Overseers accounts for Felsham record a payment to 'Mrs Orams for soap to wash the linen and bed-ticks after the people having the Smallpox'. Surely an outbreak of smallpox would have been noteworthy. This is one of a number of surprising omissions from the journal. In October 1833, William Tate and Henry Johnson were transported for stealing silver spoons, a diamond ring and two sovereigns from a Thorpe Morieux farmer named William Newson. In March 1836, James Osborne was transported for stealing cheeses and pullets from Benjamin Smith of Thorpe Green. Both robberies were within half a mile of where William Scarfe lived, yet he did not mention them. However, one page from the prayer book has been lost, and maybe that is where he wrote about stories like this.

Brought sum applelsimes of my fathers stock
(The young apple stems for grafting were known as scions.
We presume this is what he meant.)

1831 Apr 27 Wm Scarfe of Thorpe was Born . . .

1831 May 22 . . . Recived in the Church

1831 Jul 10 Some popel played *(or 'flayed')* the kage of ouer
cart and Rope G Andres found It

1831 Jul 23 Mr Joel Rakers of Hessett give Mary Scarfe a Pig
Brought it to Thorpe
(Joel Raker was married to William Scarfe's niece.)

1831 Jul 27 Lost our old Mer 29 Brok the Arme of our cart the
coult soon Died fell of the cart as I was a Loding
it in Thorpe Wood

1831   Mr John Scarfe Carted our Hudles to fornham

(With their cart broken, their mare dead and an order to deliver, it seems it was 'brother to the rescue again'. Hurdle-making appears to have been William Scarfe's main money earner.)

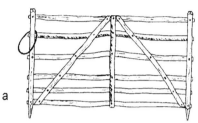

a

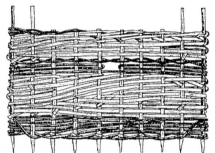

b

Hurdle-Making

The traditional Suffolk Hurdle was a gate hurdle (a). It was light and was about 6 foot long by 4 foot high. A number could be easily carried and could be driven into the ground, or more commonly supported by posts known as shores. Gate Hurdles were usually made from riven ash, and were primarily used for penning sheep. The hurdle maker may also have made wattle hurdles (b), weaving hazel rods around ash poles.

1831   Wm Scarfe and is son Wm Harvesed at Mr George Grimwade of Thorpe

1831 Aug 7   Wm Scarfe whent to Hessett with our couls To weome *(welcome?)* With Mr Joel Rakers couls.

(As a woodman, the production of charcoal may have been part of William Scarfe's work. Even if it was not, woodmen would have been followed, as they progressed through the woods, by charcoal burners. The photograph below shows a 19th century charcoal burner living with his family in the woods he worked. The coals William Scarfe mentions may have referred to charcoal produced in Thorpe and Felsham Woods.)

1831 Aug 7   Wm Horkings Died at Cockfield at wm Tylers
(He was buried, aged 84, at Cockfield 12th August 1831.)

1831 Aug   In the month of August old John Howard was very ill he Could not make water the Docter had to D*(r)*aw it
(He lived another ten years. Also, he wasn't that old – just 59 at this date.)

1831 Sep 9   the 9 Curnl Cormac wife was Bured at Brettenham

(Henrietta Camac, aged 44, wife of Col. John Camac, 1st Life Guards. The Camac family resided at Brettenham Hall at the time.)

Troubled times at Brettenham Hall

Henrietta Camac, before marriage, was the last legitimate member of the Wenyeve family, who had held the Brettenham estate for centuries. Her marriage and subsequent occupation of the Hall brought inheritance claims from other parts of the family. For much of the early nineteenth century, the estate was held in Chancery and even before John Camac's death, in a desperate attempt to make the estate pay, parts of the hall were let to tenants such as Captain Nisbett, whose death followed soon after Henrietta's.

Brettenham Hall in the nineteenth century

1831 Sep 11   Isaac Scarfe was Desey by Running Rond Sceared is Mother she Thought he had ben an died we was All Scared to se Him

1831 Sep 16   Bought our New Meare at Woolpit faire Jipsey by Name Mr John Scarfe of Hessett paid for the meare the price as 7 pound

(White's Directory for 1844 describes Woolpit having an annual fair for cattle and toys on 19th September.)

Provincial fairs

Provincial fairs like the one at Woolpit had a very bad reputation, with just cause, as this article from the London Morning Post *for 1820 shows:*

'At Woolpit fair on Saturday the 16th there was a great show of horses, but little business done. At the cattle fair on Tuesday and Wednesday, the supply of beasts was good, both as to quantity and quality; but of these also the sale was very dull. The fair was as usual infested with swindlers, and more than usually atrocious frauds were committed by a gang of villains, who set up at Beyton Bear for three days, and passed a number of Country bank notes, altered from 1L to 10L and others purporting to be issued from banks which never had any existence, or had failed. They paid three of these at the above public-house, one at the White Horse, and got rid of the others for change. They also purchased a horse with one, and passing through Bury on Saturday afternoon, bought a bridle of Mr. Partridge, in the Southgate-street, receiving 9L as change for an altered note. The owner of the horse pursued them to Bury, when Mr. Markham, of the Angel Inn, with some of his servants, followed the villains on horse-back; but though he at one time very nearly got up with them near Hengrave, they escaped, and reached Brandon, where the owner (some delay having taken place in Bury) did not arrive till next morning, when he found they had slept there. At Shouldham Fair, on Tuesday, similar frauds were committed, and a man was apprehended, who had upon him upwards of 400L in good notes, and we understand he has been identified, and committed to Norwich Castle.'

1831 Sep 16   Mr Neslby Died at Brettenham Hall was Bured
In Brettenham Church by Mr Coale Rector of the
parish

*(This must be John Alexander Nisbett Esq., late of the 1st
Life Guards, who died aged 21. The* Suffolk Herald *gives a
rather heartless account of his death.)*

> **MELANCHOLY DEATH OF CAPTAIN NISBETT.**
> —Last Friday three weeks, as Captain Nisbett, of
> Brettenham Hall, late of the Guards, was trying
> a horse in harness down the North Hill, at Col-
> chester, the animal set off at full speed, and the
> reins breaking, Captain N., in attempting to get
> out, was thrown down and severely injured. His
> face and head were cut, and he was a good deal
> bruised; but the injury inflicted on the knee-pan
> was the ultimate cause of his death,—which was
> so dreadfully shattered that mortification ensued,
> and he died on Friday last, just three weeks after
> the accident occurred. He was in the habit of
> driving at a furious rate, and it is almost a matter
> of surprise, that no accident sooner occurred.
> This gentleman, it will be in the recollection of
> our readers, married Miss Mordaunt, of Drury
> Lane Theatre; he was but 21 years of age, and
> his widow is barely yet 19.

1831 Sep 18   John Risby was Bured at Brettenham

*(The Brettenham burial register names him as Richard
Risby, age 72.)*

1831 Sep 19   begun to fell in Felsham wood for our selves
Simon Last had the first Hudles that whe Made
Brettenham

*(He makes the clear distinction between working to sell to
others and felling to supply themselves. Almost certainly,
his workers were paid in kind for this piece of felling. Also,
time would have been set aside for supplying their tithe to
the vicar. In 1831, this could still have been paid in kind.*

*After 1843, when the tithe revision came to Thorpe, William
Scarfe's tithe was assessed at £9 2s 0d in total for working
Thorpe, Felsham and Hastings Woods.)*

When to fell?

*John Evelyn wrote that hazel cutting should begin when
the nut is loose in the husk (September) and should always
finish by Lady Day (25th March). By tradition, these times
were closely adhered to.*

Gate hurdles, still in use at West Stow

1831 Oct 12   Old Mr Farnley of Felsham Died aged 82 He was
Bured at Felsham on the 18

*(Samuel Farnley is shown in the Felsham parish
register to be 84.)*

1831 Oct

John Bird at the Folley Farm Thorpe Mary North Lidy Wittel theay borth ware Hose Keepers for him are Boath in the familey way by ther Master John Bird Lidy Wittel be Long to London Mary North be Long to Thorpe John Bird be Long to Brettenham

(John Bird, recently widowed, found himself in a dilemma. He seems to have resolved it by marrying one of them. John and Lydia Bird baptised their son John at Brettenham on 15th March 1832. In the 1851 census, Liddy Bird gives her birthplace as Malden, Essex.)

1831 Nov 25

a Deep snow fell and Larsted for 10 weeks

1831 Nov 27

James Smith of felsham was Bured by the felsham Club 38 pursons attend him to the Buriel Lost his Life by weathin *(wearing?)* a silver gurdle for the Itch

(He was 45. The Mysterious 'itch' commonly appears in newspaper adverts of the time. All kinds of cures were on offer for 'the itch'.)

1831 Nov 27

James Smith of felsham was Bured by the felsham Club 40 porsons attend him corst for his funel 7 13 0

1831 Dec

In the month of Deember 1831 Sarah Tayler Died in London

1832 Jan 2

Mr Wm Borlden of Cockfield a farmer Hung him self Bured at Thorpe

(William Baldwin, aged 64, was buried on 7th January.)

1832 Jan 11

Thos and Daniel Simons of felsham was Tried for Robbing of Mr G Keridge of Felsham Thos 2 years Inprisonment Daniel 1 yeare prinsement

(The Bury & Norwich Post *for 18th January reports the two
Symonds brothers being found guilty of stealing 5 coombs of
barley. At Bury Quarter Sessions, Daniel Symonds, aged 27,
and Thomas Symonds, 35, received the above sentences with
hard labour.)*

Hard Labour!

*The Bury Gaol had been pupose built in 1805 and extended
in 1819. Within the confines of one of its buildings, aptly
named the House of Correction, a Tread Mill had been
constructed, in which 80–100 men could work at one time in
four different rooms, according to the category of prisoner.
They were employed in grinding corn and were allowed to
keep two fifths of their earnings.*

1832 Jan 22   John Howard mob Mr John Stearn in the Church
yard concearning his Boay Behaving bad In the
Church

1832 Feb 1   John Bird whent to Live In Scotts Howse Ranger *(?)* Brettenham

1832 Feb 5   Bought A pig of Mr Fred Melton 1 0 0 from Mrs Garnham farm at Thorpe Morriuex

1832 Mar 8   Bengham Smith wageon fell In to the Mr Sparkes Ditch Loding with Sand for Mr Absen *(Arbon?)* of Thorp

Wagon accidents seem to have been so common because of the practice of riding on the shafts. However, many of these waggons were little more than two pairs of wheels and left little room for the driver.

1832 Mar 12   Wm Listers Boay was found Ded in his bed he was trubled with fits
(John Lister, aged 13, was buried at Thorpe on 18th March.)

1832 Mar 16   Susan Crick was Confined with A fine Boay his Name is Walter the son of Edw Crick this makes her13 children Mrs Scarfe put her to bed

1832 Mar 21   a farst Day for the Ch-removers *(?)*

(This strange word has been hard to place. Newspapers of the time write about a Fast Day for the poor which was hijacked by mass protests in London where 20,000 protesters fought with 4,000 police. There was stone throwing and batons were drawn. Being the Wednesday after Ash Wednesday that year, it was designated an Ember Day.)

1832 Mar 29   Jothen Stevens of Thorpe Died

(Jonathan Stevens, aged 76, was buried at Thorpe on 6th April.)

1832 Mar 31   Wm Gladwell of felsham Died he was a thatcher

(He was 84, buried at Felsham on 14th April.)

1832 Mar   George Howard wife was Confined with Boay she had the Ager

(This is probably Henry Haward, son of George and Frances Haward, baptised at Thorpe 4th August 1833. The name Howard/Haward/Hayward appears in a variety of forms. As today, children were not always baptised straight away unless they were not expected to survive. Some families baptised clusters of children at the same time.)

1832 Mar   Wm Grimard whent Shrofted farie at Lavenham Lorst sum money He lived Brettenham

(White's directory describes a Shrovetide Tuesday Fair at Lavenham. There are many newspaper accounts of theft from Lavenham and other fairs. See the entry for 12th February 1839.)

1832 Mar   in the Month of March A young Man Hung Himself at Lavenham He frinds Lived at Ewsen fox He was a printes *(apprentice)* to a Grocer at Lavenham

(Ewsen may mean Edwardstone. Alternatively, it could refer to Euston in the north of the county, or Ousden to the West.

*These were both some way distant, but both did have a
public house called The Fox.)*

'Man Splitting Stakes' by Harry Becker

1832 Apr 19 Mrs Harrison of Thorpe was Confined with a Gall
She was taken in her Labour at Copford Hall in
Essex at Mager Harrisons
*(The child was called Elizabeth and was baptised at Thorpe
on this date.)*

1832 Apr 23 begun to peel Barke In Thorpe wood an . . .

1832 Apr 26 . . . It rained A good Deel whe Could not work

1832 Apr 28 Master Greens Daughter Died In Decline come
from Bury
*(Probably Harriet Green, aged 21, buried at Thorpe on 2nd
May.)*

1832 Apr 29 Robert Treasey was Taken very Ill he got Tipsey
at Isaac Barrelles Brettenham
*(Isaac Barrell was keeper of the beer-house at
Brettenham.)*

1832 Apr 29 the tow Littel Twins whent to Church the first time

1832 May   Old May Day It Snowed And Rained whe ment to go to Hessett fro Thorpe Morrieux

1832 May 1   Thorpe Morriuex May 1 Cockfield faire

1832 May 1   It Rained verey Hard

1832 May 25   Mrs Bixby of felsham Baker Died
(Elizabeth Bixby, aged 68, was buried at Felsham on 30th May.)

1832 Jun 9   Fred Mays foute with Stephen Harper for five shillings Stephen Harper Bate foute at Wm Greens Brettenham Samul How was Ill at that time He Lost Some time
(A little later, in 1841, Stephen Harper lived up on the Cockfield Road by the Boundary Stone, where to this day, a stone marks the meeting point of Cosford, Thedwastre and Thingoe Hundreds. There are numerous newspaper accounts of prize-fights at this time. Some resulted in serious injury or even death.)

1832 Jun 10   It Thunard on Wisensunday June 10 It Rained a good Deal It was a Durty Day for to go A Horledy Making being horledy time

1832 Jun 10   Beny Green And Mrs Harrisons Nuss *(nurse)* Maid whent to Bury St Edmunds on Wisen Sunday for to make Harledy

1832 Jun 11   The Littel Twines whent to Hessett to se John Raker whe All whent from Thorpe

1832 Jun 30   Wm Sturgeon from Bradfield Manger Come to Thorpe to se Wm Scarfe

(This may be the Bradfield Manger public house, or maybe he means the village of Bradfield Combust – William Sturgeon does not appear to have been a publican.)

1832 Jun   Mr Anderson prashed *(preached)* From Felsham for Mr Harrison

1832 Jul 12   Whe had a Tempes it Litened very much Buxhall Mill was Hurt from the Thorpe Tempest this Day Raine was not very much finished Hudle Making in Thorpe Wood

(Buxhall Mill was a wooden smock mill, which had been built in 1815 by Samuel Wright, a miller from Ipswich. It replaced an earlier post mill, which had burnt down. Following the damage it received from 'the Thorpe Tempest,' Buxhall Mill was never wholly satisfactorily repaired and was replaced thirty years later by a brick tower mill, the remains of which can be seen to this day.)

The diary of Thomas King, miller of Thelnetham in Suffolk (1804–1838) is held at the Suffolk Record Office at Bury St Edmunds (ref. 920.KIN). Being a miller, he is particularly interested in high winds and, like William Scarfe, uses the word 'Tempest' a good deal. Of 12th July 1832, he writes: 'sails blown off Pakenham mill in a sharp thunderstorm'. See also the entries for the end of July 1834 and March 1837.)

1832 Jul 26   Broke the Arme of our Cart Loded with 30 Lits
(See the entry for 27th July 1840 for a possible interpretation of the word 'Lits'.)

1832 Aug 13   Mr John Scarfe and Mrs Raker from Hessett came to Thorpe to our House

Contemporary engravings of woodmen working.

1832 Aug 17 Robert Offord wife of Thorpe Died Left 2
Children
*(Susan Offord, aged 36, was buried at Thorpe on 21st
August 1832.)*

1832 In 1832 had to take Hay and corn for the Harvest
of Mr George Grimwad of Thorpe
*(A confusing discovery has been a newspaper advertisement
for October 1829 describing the sale particulars of George
Grimwade's farm at Thorpe Morieux. Either he did not sell,
or he must have moved to another farm in Thorpe.)*

1832 Sep 7 begun to fell in felsham Wood
*(At no point does William Scarfe talk of coppicing, though it
is hard to believe this was not an important part of his work
as a woodman. He appears to use the expression 'felling'
to describe the cutting of coppice as well as the felling of
larger oaks for later bark-peeling.)*

1832 Oct 10 Mrs Rafe of Felsham Died in Decline

Poles and brushwood left after coppicing in Combs Wood.

Deep in Thorpe Wood

1832 Oct 27   ower cart whent to Hayham *(this could mean Higham)* For Jospeh Stearnes things Brought them to Bradfield St Clare Suffolk

1832 Nov 10   Mr John Scarfe of Hessett his BurthDay born the 10 of November Whe All whent to se him

1832 Dec 3   John Didins Labour fell Down Broke his Leg ben to Lavenham got Drunk fell Down in Thorpe Rode

1832   Mary North Child Died

(She was the one who did not marry the father of her child – see the entry regarding John Bird, October 1831.)

1832   Mrs Crick is in the familey way this make 11 Children

(The entry for 16th March 1832 seems to suggest this was her 13th child, though it was only the tenth to be baptised at Thorpe.)

1833 Jan 1   Wm Northe marridaged to Mary Ann Mudd of Thorpe

1833 Feb 13   Jack Horlex Died the Night before valenting Day feb 13 at Gedding

(This is almost certainly Zachariah Horrex, aged 60, buried at Felsham; see next entry.)

1833 Feb 17   Jack Horlex was Bured at felsham Died at Gedding

1833 Feb 18   Mrs Harrison confined the Child is Ded

(Charles Harrison, infant, was buried at Thorpe)

1833 Mar 26   the 26 good Deal of snow fell

1833 Mar 31 Mr John Scarfe from Hessett was to come to
Thorpe to Let us Know ABout given notes to
have our House be Longing to Mr Thos Sparke of
Thorpe Morriuex Suffolk

*Here is the first indication that his brother is about to buy
him a house.*

Moat Farm Cottage as it is today

1833 Apr 4 old Mr Maidell Died at felsham Lived In Mr
Morgan House he have ben Blind for Time

*(Thomas Maidwell, aged 86, was buried at Gedding on 3rd
April 1833.)*

1833 Apr 10 The 10 Saml Rush of Thorpe Died Bured on the Sunday after Ester taken coming fom Wm North

(He was 70, buried at Thorpe on 14th April. Samuel Rush the blacksmith had been to visit William North, carpenter and wheelwright, demonstrating the interdependence of the craftsmen of the village.)

1833 Apr 15 John Bramford when to Prison for steling of Barley from Simon Last of Brettenham

(According to the Court Records, John Bramford, aged 31, received six months hard labour, with the last week to be spent in solitary confinement.)

1833 Apr 15 Warterman of Brettenham had his Malt Taken away his Kell pould Down by the superviser and the Exsiman

(This sounds as though he was operating a still. Although a kell more commonly meant a kiln, the book Larn Yarself Silly Suffolk *describes a kell as associated with brewing.)*

1833 May 5 Mr Melton and Wm Scarfe Whent to felsham Church

1833 May 18 Whe Loded A loade of Barke out of Hassen Wood

The wood William Scarfe calls Hassen Wood is known as Great Hastings Wood and is still coppiced to this day

(One of the nearest tanneries was at Combs near Stowmarket. It is known from surviving documentation that they were buying bark from the Thorpe area at 3s 6d a fathom. The tannin from the bark was what gave 'tanning' its name and enabled hide to be turned into leather.)

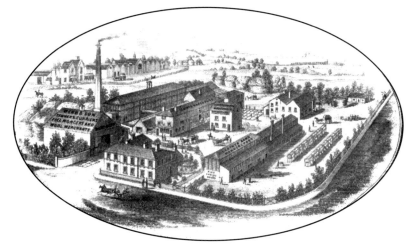

This notice was once displayed at the gate of the tannery. The 'Bait' referred to was hay and water for the horse.

COMBS TANNERY
NEAR STOWMARKET.

NOTICE.

All Persons bringing Bark to these Premises are requested to Remain on the Road side of the Weigh Bridge till their turn comes for Weighing and Unloading, and all Persons found on the other side of the Entrance Gate, without an order, will not be entitled to a Bait.

WEBB & SON.

Smoking on any part of these Premises entirely Prohibited.

1833 May   In may begun to peel Bark in Hasing Wood *(Hastings Wood)* John Bird Wm Scarfe John North

1833 May 19 Edward Howlett of Bayton Come to Thorpe to
oure House Broght some money for Brotches
He ored sum Brotches to be Rove He Come the
Sunday Before WisenSunday

*(Howlett was another woodman who turned his hand to a bit
of thatching in the Summer months. Riving was the splitting
of the hazel stems using a riving-hook. William Scarfe seems
to have had a busy trade, producing the brotches which
thatchers used to secure the thatch. Surprisingly, there is no
mention of William Nice, a near-neighbour who was also a
thatcher. Presumably Mr Nice prepared his own brotches.)*

1833 May 25 ower Cart whent to Bayton with a Loade of
Brotches the Sunday before Wisensunday

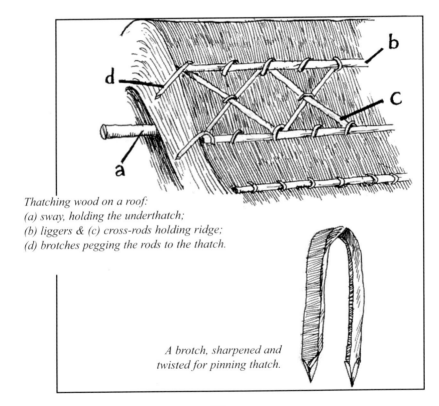

Thatching wood on a roof:
(a) sway, holding the underthatch;
(b) liggers & (c) cross-rods holding ridge;
(d) brotches pegging the rods to the thatch.

*A brotch, sharpened and
twisted for pinning thatch.*

In May Wm Pilbrow fought with George Todd of felsham at the Beds

(These could have been osier beds, where willow was grown for basket weaving, although John Squirrell, local history recorder for Thorpe, has pointed out that there used to be an area in the Rectory garden where the game of quoits was played. This was known as the 'Quoit Beds'.)

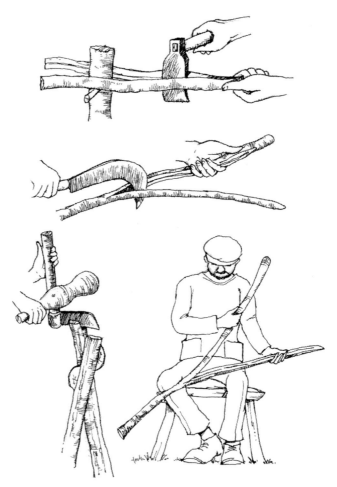

Riving wood – splitting hazel rods by hand or with an assortment of tools

1833 May   In the month of may a grate meney pepel Are
taken Ill with a favour

(This is not reflected in the local burials which are no higher than normal. See the entry for February 1837.)

1833 May   In the month of may Wm Payne farmer Broke his
Leg A man at Bayton had his Arme Bit by a Stalyen
be Longing to Mr Worpool of Bayton Suffolk

(William Walpole Esq. of Beyton Lodge)

1833 Jun 1   paid Edward Crick 8 Shillings for his Boay Tom
for work

1833 Jun 2   Bought a pig of George Howard

1833 Jun 7   Bought 2 pigs 1 10s of Mr Spark

1833 Jun 8   Wm wife paid for theare Half a hund of Wood
1 9 0

1833 Jun 8   Ann Pilbrow was Bured at Brettenham Cared
In a Hearse from felsham She was taken with A
Infathon *(infection)*

(Entered in the parish register as Elizabeth Pilbrow, aged 51.)

1833 Jun 12   Maria Scarfe was confined with fine Boy at
Thorpe his name is called Fredrick

(Fredrick was crossed out)

1833 Jun 12   Jacob Scarfe was Boarn Recived in to the Church
July 14 the Son of Maria Scarfe of Thorpe the
Daughter of James Boggies of felsham

(Possibly christened Jacob Frederick.)

1833 Jun   In the month of June Mr Sparkes maid had A
young Child and it Deded

1833 Jun 20   Mr Thos Sparkes maid lost A Child Lizar Bran
(Lisa Brown?)

1833 Jun 22   Joseph Goold Died of Thorpe taken Ill the 18
work at Mr John Stearns farmer at the folley farm
(He was 58 and was buried at Thorpe and 25th June.)

1833 Jun 23   the 23 Mr Harrison toke his Text In the 24 Chapter
of Matthew on the count of Jospeh Goold being
taken of In a Hurrey ye Know not wot ower the
son of man Cometh

1833 Jun 29   Thos Smith and Wm Scarfe whnt to Mr Daves for
the Intres money for the felsham Club One hund
and sixty pound at 4 per sent Mr Wolten have got
50 pound

The Felsham Club Accounts

If this is the interest, then the club must have had in the region of £4,000 on account. Original feelings were that 'Mr. Daves' must refer to a Banker in Bury St Edmunds and this may be so, but another possibility is that either Charles Davers, gentleman, of Felsham or Rev. Robert Davers, Rector of Rougham and Lord of the Manor at Bradfield St George, may have been their independent financial adviser. When the West Suffolk Friendly Society was formed in 1830, a number of local parsons were trustees.

1833 Jul 7 Mr John Scarfe of Hessett Gave his Brother Wm the House he Bought of Mr Shoman Ded be Long to Mr farnley of felsham

(Mr Pearson Sharman was the executor of Mr Farnley's will and therefore responsible for the sale of his assets. He appears listed in White's directory for 1844 as a miller in Great Barton near Bury. Samuel Farnley had died in October 1831.)

1833 In the year of 1833 Mr John Scarfe of Hessett Bought the Howse beLong to Mr Sharman at Barton it was Mr farleys Mr John Scarfe of Hessett bought whe a house

1833 Jul 14 Jacob Scarfe was Named and Chrisned Mrs Boggies stod for him at the folley Farm

(These last two lines appear close together in the journal but may not belong together. The suggestion is that Mrs Boggis was Jacob's godmother.)

1833 Jul 22 John Parmer Maria Howard was marided at Thorpe Chrisned young Child

(In the parish register for Thorpe, they appear as John Palmer and Maria Hayward. They married on 23rd July and baptised a daughter, Sarah, at Thorpe on 8th June 1834. In 1841, John Palmer lived almost opposite William Scarfe.)

1833 Jul 26 Bengham Levett marred to Elizabeath How of Thorpe

(Benjamin Levett and Elizabeth Howe married at Brettenham.)

1833 Wm Scarfe Harves with his Brother John at Hessett And he Keept ower Meare Jipsey by Name

1833 Aug 7   Mr John Scarfe hurt him self by fallingout of the cart over Meare Jipsey *(the mare, 'Gypsy')*

1833 Aug 16 old Mr Raker and his wife was at Hessett at Mr John Scarfes to Diner

(John Scarfe's daughter was married to Joel Raker)

1833 Aug 31 Mrs Leepope was Bured Hessett Brought from London Hearse And 6 Horses A Coach and 4 Horses

(Ann Leheup, aged 42, was buried 1st August 1833, wife of Michael Leheup Esq. – see the entry for December 1837.)

1833 Sep 7   finished Harvest Hessett for Mr John Scarfe

This early haymaking photograph taken from the Scarfe family collection, though clearly posed, shows how haymaking and harvesting were something the whole family would be involved in.

William Scarfe's cottage at Thorpe Morieux. He and his wife occupied one end and William Scarfe Junior with wife and children lived in the other end.

1833 Oct 12   Wm Scarfe and his son moved into his New House at Thorpe

(This was Moat Farm Cottage, which still stands opposite the Village Hall in Thorpe.)

1833 Nov 26   Mrs Sparke the wife of Thos Sparke Deded of Thorpe once was a Shomaker at Thorpe Suffolk

(Sarah Sparke, aged 92, was buried at Thorpe on 1st December 1833; Thomas was 17 years younger.)

1833 Dec 5   Edward Howlett come to Thorpe to oder sme Brotches

1833 Dec 8   George Howard come And paid his Bill

1834 Jan 4   Mr John Stearn and Wm Scarfe fell out in Hassings wood

(This was probably not a good idea on William's part. John

Stearn was principal resident landowner in Thorpe and as can be seen regarding the 1837 election, was a man of influence in the village. See the entry for August 1837.)

1834 Jan 5   had 2 pigs of James Sadler 1 1 0

1834 Jan 16   Ben Morgan Died at Rattelsden with the favour
(fever)

(Benjamin Morgan, aged 61, was buried at Rattlesden on 21st January 1834.)

1834 Jan   In the month of Janry M Dyer Had a Child Laid to him

(A young farmer by the name of William Dyer lived close by. Alternatively, William Scarfe may mean Diaper, which was a commoner name in the area. Unfortunately, far fewer of Thorpe's parish records survive than do Felsham's, and there are no surviving bastardy orders for Thorpe Morieux.)

1834 Jan   Miss Susan Arbon Died in Jan 1834 at Rattelsden Bured at felsham

(Aged 60, buried 9th January 1834.)

1834 Jan   In the month of Janry Robert Treasey and his wife was very Ill of Thorpe Suffolk

1834 Jan   In the month of January whe had our Singing frolock at our House Mr Harrison gave ten Shillings

1834 Jan   In the month of Janry Mr Fredrick Meltens Wife was Confined at Thorpe

(The child was Orlando Melton, born to Frederic Rands Melton (farmer) and his wife Frances. Baptised on February 22nd at Thorpe, the child died at just 23 weeks. The Meltons buried eight children in infancy.)

1834 Feb 25   Wm Listers wife was Bured at Thorpe

(Elizabeth Lister, aged 36)

1834 Mar 16   Wm Lister went a Courting to Bet Bird

(Now see the entry for April 13th.)

1834 Mar 22   finish Brushing In Hassings Wood

Brushwood used to create fencing around a newly coppiced area to protect the new shoots from forest animals.

1834 Mar 30   In the month of March 30 Henery Grimwood
was taken Ill Died on the 14 of April Lived at the
folley farm 42 yeares Buried on the 20 of April
Meny poopel Foled Him

(Henry Grimwood, aged 68, was buried at Thorpe.)

1834 Apr 10   John Andres Died at Reede He be Long to the
felsham Club

(Aged 43, buried 14th April at Rede.)

1834 Apr 13   *(Wm Lister)* was published in the Church to Bet
Bird

*(The banns were read, and his first wife only buried six
weeks earlier.)*

1834 Jul 7   Fredwick Allington come to Thorpe from London
The Son of Jospeh Allington from London

The ancient craft of brashing

*What William Scarfe calls 'brushing', some modern wood-
men refer to as 'brashing'. After hazel, ash and alder were
coppiced, long stems began to grow from the base. To
achieve a substantial thickness of poles, side shoots were
removed using a hook or brashing tool. The aim was to
produce good smooth straight poles; the finished product
was a source of pride for the experienced woodman. Such
poles were often used for rake handles. Alternatively, brush
or brash was cut from the poles that had been felled and
bundled up into faggots or made into dead wood fencing
around the newly coppiced stools. This was to protect the
young shoots from deer and other forest animals. Brushing
was done in late Spring or early Summer before the nettles
and brambles became too dense.*

1834 Jul 15   The Wife of Joseph Aves of Thorpe was found Ded in her Bed

(Martha Aves, aged 53, died on 16th July and was buried at Thorpe on 21st July 1834. She was the daughter of William Gault of Little Whelnetham.)

1834 Jul 21   be gun Harvest at Hessett for Mr John Scarfe

1834 Jul 27   It was a Butufull fine Harvest the whate was very fine Lasted but a Littel Time July 27 Rote

1834 Jul   Wm Scarfe Sn Harvested at Hassett Suffolk Begun in July finished Augest 13

1834 Jul   In the Month July whe Had a Tempes it Rained very Hard it Litened very much at Thorpe

---

A stormy summer

Ours is not the only diary to mention this stormy summer. The diary of Thomas King, miller of Thelnetham, describes how at the end of a long hot July, the storms broke:

'Redenhall Steeple struck by lightning and hurt July 1834'
'Market Weston steeple struck by lightning July 19th 1834'
'Sharp lightning July 28 1834 a barn burnt at North Lopham'
'A very sharp tempest July 31 1834 ruin and hurt done at Travers Fair. Diss mill shattered. Barn at Billingford House and lands struck. 30 acres wheat burnt'

1834 Sep 2   Fredrick Allington Set of for London from Ipswich by a steem Packet

1834 Sep 18   begun to fell in Felsham wood

THE IPSWICH STEAM COMPANY most respectfully inform the Public that their fast and commodious

STEAM PACKET,

"IPSWICH,"

CAPTAIN CHARLES WING,

Will continue her Voyages, Twice a Week, between Ipswich and London, calling off Harwich, Walton-on-the-Naze, and Southend.

The Vessel will leave Mr. Seekamp's Wharf, Ipswich, every Monday and Thursday Morning, (instead of Tuesday and Friday) at 7 o'clock precisely, and return from St. Catharine's Wharf, London, every Tuesday and Friday Morning, (instead of Wednesday and Saturday) at the above time.

FARES.

Chief Cabin .... 8s. 6d.
Fore Ditto....................... 6s. 0d.
From Ipswich to Harwich ...,.....2s. 0d.
Ditto to Walton-on-the-Naze......3s. 0d.

Children under Ten Years of age at Half-price.

Refreshments may be had, and a Stewardess will be on board.—The Vessel will always start precisely at the time stated above, and the Captain is not accountable for Luggage.

For further particulars apply as under.

IPSWICH.

At the Sea Horse, Bull, or Crown and Sceptre Inns, Common Quay; at Mr. Seekamp's Counting House; at the Rose Inn, St. Peter's; at the Bell Inn, or the Life Boat, Stoke.

An advertisement from a Suffolk Chronicle *of the time*

An anonymous journal of this time, entitled 'An Outline of Proceedings for Every Day of the Year', covers events in the Stowmarket area 1834–1838. Its author comments:

'July 29th – A most wonderful and awful night of thunder & lightning which done considerable damage, especially at Woodbridge, one house burnt down by electric fluid.'

'August 2nd – Such hot weather hardly ever known by the oldest persons living

'August 2nd – Finished wheat harvest

'August 11th – Finished barley harvest

'August 16th – Finished bean harvest'

1834 Sep 13   toke in a pece of Grownd to our Garden by order of Mr Jossylen Stward

(Mr Josselyn was Steward for Henry Sparrow Esq., who was Lord of the Manor of Thorpe but lived at Gosfield in Essex. This sounds very like the establishment of an allotment.)

Allotments

Two local figures at this time were strong advocates of allocating small pieces of land at much reduced rents to enable the poor of their parishes to add to their meagre incomes. Sir Henry Bunbury at Great Barton and Rev. Professor Henslow at Hitcham pioneered the cultivation of allotments, believing, with some justification, it would provide profit for the deserving poor and cut down on crime caused by 'idleness and poverty'. The Court of Guardians in Bury resolved in 1834 'to apportion parcels of land to enable the industrious poor to cultivate by means of spade-husbandry upon the priciples recommended by the Labourers' Friend Society'.

CONDITIONS.

1.   The Rent to be paid punctually on Old Michaelmas Day; half the Rent to be paid in advance.

2.   The Land to be cultivated with the spade only, and to be well manured, and no Dogs to be brought upon the ground.

3.   No Crop to occupy more than half the allotment, (as laid out in the plan) and a third of the allotment to be with corn every year.

4.   No work to be done on the allotments on Sundays.

5.   No Tenant is to re-let or exchange any part of his allotment.

6.   The Tenants must agree to prevent depredations on each others allotments.

7.   Every kind of encroachment to be strictly avoided ; and should any individual be guilty of theft or other misdemeanor, he will be subject to an immediate ejectment, without the slightest remuneration for labour or planting.

8.   Any Tenant to assist in detecting and convicting persons who may be guilty of destroying or injuring property.

9.   As the object in letting this land is to improve the conditions of the occupiers ; and being convinced that it is impossible to do do those any real or lasting good who live irreligiously, it is required of all the Tenants that they, with their families, attend the Parish Church regularly ; send their Children to school ; abstain from drunkenness and swearing ; and endeavour, through God's help, to live in all things as becometh Christians.

Remember, All the above Conditions are so necessary, that they who wilfully break them will not be permitted to hire their Allotments again ; and those who do not Cultivate their Land properly, will be required to give it up.

I, *William Tybon* agree to hire of the *Feoffees of Felsham, from the 11* day of October, 18 3 9 to the 11 day of

Though we were unable to trace an allotment contract for Thorpe, this list of conditions for Felsham dates from 1839.

1834 Sep 18   Mrs Scarfe whent to Bayton come Home by Hessett

1834 Sep 25   Miss Bixby of felsham Died was Burred on the 25 she Lived at felsham Hall

(Elizabeth Bixby, aged 55.)

Oct 22   Ann Making whent to Live with Mr Green

(Maria-Ann Makin later married William Green at Preston St Mary, 18th March 1835. Trial marriages were alive and well in 1834.)

1834 Nov 2   James Sparke Died at Thorpe come from London

(Aged 71, he was buried on 6th November at Thorpe.)

1835 Jan 1   Joseph Allington at London Brother to Mary Scarfe of Thorpe he Died on 1 Jan at London

1835 Jan 7   begun in Thorpe Wood

'Trees' by Harry Becker

1835 Jan 8   finish in felsham Wood

1835 Jan 26   Wido Crick of Thorpe Died taken at 2 oclock in morning Died at 1 Afternoon
(Mary Crick, aged 74, was buried at Thorpe on 1st February 1835.)

1835 Feb 12   Mrs Crick was Confined with a fine Boay
(Frederick)

1835 Feb 22   Mr Mudd Died was Ill for long Doter Gedding
(Francis David Mudd, aged 65, was buried at Gedding on 3rd March 1835. Highly respected, he had been the local doctor for a number of years, having joined his father, Richard Mudd, in the Gedding practice in 1794. He was twice President of the Suffolk Benevolent Medical Society. A William Mudd is listed as a surgeon in Hadleigh in White's directory for 1844. Barrington Richard Mudd, at the age of 15, is listed in the 1841 Census for Gedding as a medical student. Doctors tended to go in families.)

1835 Feb 23   Mrs Farnley was Bured at felsham
(Anne Farnley, who was aged 78.)

1835 Feb   In the month of february James Boggies Jn wife died at felsham
(She was aged 34, and was buried at Felsham on 6th February 1835.)

1835 Apr 10   George Boggies of felsham Marrided at Fimbrow to Charlotte
(George Bogges married Charlotte Lunn at Little Finborough.)

1835 Apr 11   Finished Brushing In Thorpe wood

This rare early photograph of a bark stack at Combs Tannery gives a clear impression of the vast amount of oak bark that had to be purchased for tanning. Most of the bark was bought in April and May, and the stacks thatched to keep it dry until it was needed. The detail enlarged below shows the unloading of a cart. Bark, like wood, was sold by the fathom, one fathom being approximately six cubic feet. We know that in 1835, Webb & Son at Combs paid 3s 6d per fathom (delivered) for their bark.

1835 Apr 17   Toke in our New pece of Grownd on Good Friday
by order of Mr Jossylen
(See the entry for 13th September 1834.)

1835 Apr 23   begun to Peel Barke In Thorpe Wood the Bark
Run very Bad

The business of bark-stripping
*For about six weeks of each year, usually around April,
woodmen stripped bark from oak trees felled in the Autumn
to supply 'flaw' for the local tanneries such as the one at
Combs. Often 'hatching' – cleaning moss from the bark
– was women's work while the 'rinding' was the job of the
men. This process of stripping bark was unpredictable:
modern woodmen confirm that adjacent trees can behave
in entirely different ways – hence William Scarfe's comments about how well or how badly 'the bark runned'. Once
stripped, the bark had to be stored with its inner face down
to protect the soluble tannin from being dissolved by rain,
rendering the bark worthless.*

1835 May 19   Mrs North was Confine with a Boay
*(William, son of William North (carpenter) and his wife
Mary Ann Sarah, was baptised at Thorpe 1st January 1836.)*

1835 Aug 1   finished seeding *(?)* of Wm

1835 Aug 3   begun Harvest at Hessett

1835 Aug 10   Harvesed at Hessett begun Augest 10 finished 22

1835 *(Sept?)*   begun to fell in felsham wood

1835 Sep 29 Saml Rush And Wm Scarfe Got flung out of a
Cart at Brettenham

1835 Dec 9 Wm Scarfe Brought hom the Writings of his
House from Bury
*(He appears on the 1836 poll lists as a Freeholder of his
own property. See the entry for 4th August 1837.)*

1836 Feb 1 Recived of Eward Crick 2 Bushel of Coal from
Stowmark*(et)*

1836 Feb 7 Maria Scarfe of Thorpe Tap by Mr Robert Growse
of Bilderstone toke away 26 Points of water
*(This is the first sign that the wife of William Scarfe Junior
is seriously ill. The tapping of large volumes of water was
not unusual. An Ipswich Journal article of 1784 describes
how, over a thirty year period, a Norwich doctor was able
to tap over 6,000 pints of fluid from a woman suffering
from dropsy, so prolonging her life. However, in most cases,
tapping was never intended as a cure; it was merely to make
the patient more comfortable.)*

*__Robert Growse__ was held in high esteem in and around
Bildeston where he lived. He seems to have been referred to as
'Mr Growse the Surgeon', rarely as Dr Growse. In later life,
when his eyesight began to fail, he went to London for an eye
operation. The Suffolk Chronicle of 21st June 1864 describes
the celebrations in the village on his return. Banners were
flown, bells rung; there was music and feasting.*

1836 Feb 15 James Boggies Jn wife was confined of Felsham
*(Emily, daughter of James Boggis (labourer) and his wife
Maria was baptised at Felsham on 23rd February 1836.)*

Thorpe Morieux church from the direction of William Scarfe's cottage

1836 Feb 20   Fred Melton wife was Confined

(See entry for January 1834 – this child was christened Amelia but was buried in June.)

1836 Feb 26   George Boggis Wife was in her Laber of felsham Suffolk

(William, son of George Boggis (labourer) and Charlotte was baptised at Felsham.)

1836 Feb   In the month of Feb Mrs Rafe of felsham was confined with 2 children Mr Rafe was very Ill

(The Raffes of Felsham are listed as shopkeepers in White's directory of 1844. Members of another branch of the same family were merchants in Stowmarket.)

1836 Mar 23   Maria Scarfe was Tap By Robert Growse toke away 9 Points of water

1836 Apr 1   the first April *(Maria Scarfe)* Died 7 o clock morning toke away 45 Points of water

(Aged 40, she was buried 5th April 1836 at Thorpe.)

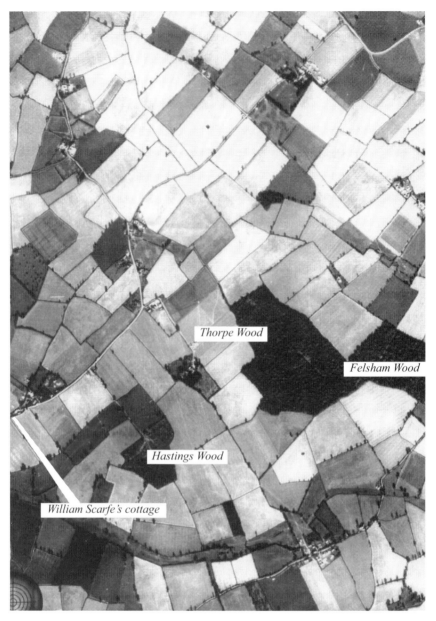

This aerial photograph was taken by the Luftwaffe just before a sizeable part of Felsham Wood was felled to ensure that planes overshooting the runway on Rattlesden airfield did not end up in the trees.

1836 May 4   begun to Peel Bark in Thorpe Wood

1836 May 5   Saml Howard S wife Died of Thorpe A month
after Maria Scafe the wife of Wm Scarfe Jnr

(Mary Howard, aged 59, was buried at Thorpe 8th May 1836.)

1836   Thatch our House the year Maria Scarfe Died the
wife of Wm Scarfe Jn of Thorpe

1836 Jun 19   Joseph aves was Publish to Mary Crick

(The banns were read.)

1836 Jul 11   Joseph Aves marrided to Mary Crick

*(At Thorpe. He was 53, she was 50. She was his second wife
– see the burial dated 15th July 1834.)*

1836 Aug 8   Whe all whent to Mr Jospeh Aves of Thorpe
Suffolk

1836 Aug 8   begun Harves at Hessett for Mr John Scarfe
fininsh Sept the 3

*(If both of these happened the same day, William Scarfe was
a fit man at 59 years of age. Joseph Aves (or Avis) lived on
the site of what is now the Bull at Thorpe. John Scarfe lived
at Hessett, six miles away.)*

1836 Sep 4   young Symons come to Thorpe

1836 Oct 13   A Dradfull Storm Come over the Hail was very
Large whe was in the wood

1836 Oct 29   Snow fell the wind was very Could

1836 Nov 27   Wm Scarfe Jn marrided to Frances Snell

(At Thorpe. It is a strange thing that marriages in the final quarter of the year far exceeded any other quarter at this time in history. The close of harvest, the termination of the year's service at Michaelmas and the festivities of the Christmas season swelled marriages to double that of any of the other quarters.)

The remarriage of widowers

There are several cases mentioned in this journal of husbands remarrying in what appears to be indecent haste following the premature death of a wife. In most cases, the women died as a result of childbirth, and parish registers of the time are full of mothers buried within days of a newly-born infant. The fact is, the widowed father of a string of children usually needed a mother for those children. William Scarfe Junior remarried just 6 months after burying his first wife. William Lister, who buried his first wife in February 1834, was courting within a month and calling the banns a month later.

1836 Dec 26   the snow was very Deep at Places the popel had to throw snow in the Rods the wind was high

1837 Jan 22   John Roberts of Thorpe Died farmer Lived in his own
(Aged 81, buried 30th January 1837.)

1837 Jan 27   Wm Wilden was Dead He was Lorst on Christmiss Day at Drinkerstone in a field be Long to Mr Jackson
(William Wilding, aged 83, was buried at Drinkstone on 29th January 1837.)

1837 Jan   in Jan whe Lost a fortnet by the Snow Thorpe

1837 Feb 8   Old Mrs Rush was Bured at Thorpe

(Sarah Rush, aged 81.)

1837 Feb 11   Mr Sparrows wagon come for Hudles from Gorsfield in Essex It rained all the Day Long

(The Sparrows of Gosfield Park near Halstead in Essex were Lords of the Manor of Thorpe Morieux.)

1837 Feb   Grate meney Popel War Ill with the Influancy feavor a Grate meny Died

(Local burials do not seem to indicate this – numbers being buried were not particularly high in the villages around Thorpe at that time. However, both local and national newspapers of the time were full of articles about the influenza epidemic. According to the Bury and Suffolk Herald *15,000 were laid up with the diease in Exeter. London and Paris were greatly affected: 80 were buried in one week at St John's Wood burial ground, Regents Park.)*

The Observer *wryly coments:*

'It is remarkable how the present epidemic has affected different orders of people in trade. Eating houses, hotels and taverns have been but scantily frequented. Butchers claim the public appetite is gone to grass. Biscuit makers and pastry cooks are doing nothing. It is not bad news for all concerned. There is unprecedented demand for licquorice, arrow-root, prunes and green tea. The chemists and druggists have shared in this harvest: and the physician who does not deign to touch anything but his patient's pulse, his prescribing pen and his fee, has pocketed many a guinea which he little expected.'

1837 Mar   Mrs John Scarfe was to come to our house the Sunday before Easter

1837 Mar 26   it Snowed Ben *(being?)* Ester Sunday the afternoon
I was to gone to Hessett

*(Thomas King's Diary relating to his experiences in
Thelnetham describes snow ten inches deep on 27th March.
The Southwold diary of James Maggs, edited by Alan
Bottomley, recounts 'a heavy fall of snow' on Easter Sunday
that year.)*

1837 Apr 16   it snowed a good Deal the Spring was very Could

1837 Apr 23   Wm Day was taken in hold for Robbery of John
Green at Mr Hustlers of Thorpe

1837 Apr 24   Wm Day was Taken up for Robing of John Green
of Thorpe and young Snell at Bildersone

*(The reports of the Bury Quarter Sessions indicate that
William Day, having been convicted of larceny, received a
12 month sentence, with three separate weeks to be in solitary confinement. It was not his first conviction. In 1835, he*

Officers bound for Australia boarding a prison hulk

had been convicted along with three others of being involved in riot and assault at Semer Workhouse. He served 12 months on that occasion too. This was not the last sentence he received.)

1837 Apr 27   finshed Brushing in Thorpe Wood

1837 Apr 30   The Las Day of April was a Blusting Day

1837   In 1837 5 of Shutlyes of Bradfield St Clare Died with favour

(There are four recorded burials for the Stuteley family at this time.)

1837 May 26   a sharpe Tempes come It rain verey Hard at Thorpe Suffolk John Raker of Brettenham had a Horse Struck Dead by Liten

1837 May 31   Settled with Mager Harrison at Tomes Harrison

(His landlord, John Haynes Harrison, was the father of the Thorpe Morieux rector, Thomas Thomas Harrison. The title

'Major' is almost certainly not a military one, unless it relates to the Essex Militia, and seems to be a courtesy title that was used for whoever was the head of the Harrison family at Cosford Hall, Essex. Manor Court records for Felsham and Thorpe accord this title to Harrison family members.)

1837 May   Begun to Peel Barke in Thorpe Wood it Rund well

1837 Jun 4   Wm Howard marred to Haner Horlex of Thorpe
(Her surname is given as Horrox in the Thorpe register.)

1837 Jun 16   Carted the Timber out of Thorpe Wood

1837 Jun 17   Mrs Harrison of Thorpe come Hom from London

1837 Jun 18   Wm Scarfe and his wife and Children went Abraham Chinerys at Rattelsden

1837 Jul 1   had a singing frolick at our House
(William Scarfe mentions this form of entertainment a lot. This is just one of many such entries, but was the only

> ### A Singing Frolic
> *It was a time of making your own entertainment. William Scarfe seems to have been a sober man who enjoyed simple pleasures. He only mentions going to the beerhouse as part of a social gathering, such as the Felsham Club. These 'singing frolics' seem to have involved meeting at the houses of members of their choir, or at the invitation of others. Occasionally, they received payment for their efforts. We can only guess what kind of songs they may have sung.*

summer reference. Most were in January when the weather must have put a stop to most other activity.)

1837 Jul 8   John Long wife of Thorpe Died at the Brick Kell Left 8 Childern

(Ann Long, aged 48, was buried at Thorpe on 12th July 1837. The Brick Kell was a brick kiln. Thorpe was not many miles from Woolpit, famed for its bricks. The Brick Kiln Cottages built in 1857 on the Lavenham Road now stand on this site.)

1837 Jul 9   Wm Scarfe went to felsham Church

1837 Jul 24   James Last Lorst a horse

1837 Jul 26   Ann Smith of Thorpe married to a man at Kersey

(This is rather confusing. An Amy Smith married Azariah Avis of Kersey in November 1837. There is no record of Ann Smith marrying either at Thorpe or Kersey.)

1837 Jul   In month of July Mr James Last was very Ill

(He was a member of the Bradfield St George Chapel which makes it more difficult to trace whether he recovered or not. Many Independent Church registers are lost.)

Making hay while the sun shone

1837 Jul   Wm Scarfe Jun went to Mr Harrisons to make Hay

1837   Wm Scarfe Harvest with Mr Dyer of Thorpe

'Scythers' by Daniel Wright

The 1837 General Election

Following a measure of electoral reform in 1832, Suffolk's 16 members of parliament were reduced to nine. The West Suffolk Constituency returned two candidates. William Scarfe (named Scarpe in the West Suffolk Poll Book for 1836) was eligible to vote by virtue of being a freeholder. Ironically, his elder brother John, who had bought his house for him, does not feature on the poll listing for his home village of Hessett. The results, announced on 7th August, were as follows:

Hart Logan *(Conservative)*	*2,217*
Col. R. Rushbrooke *(Conservative)*	*2,173*
Sir H. E. Bunbury *(Liberal)*	*1,560*
Henry Wilson *(Liberal)*	*1,505*

The farmers of West Suffolk returned two Conservative M.P.s. Sir Henry Bunbury of Great Barton, once Napoleon's gaoler and a tireless worker for the poor, lost his seat. Having topped the poll, Hart Logan died less than a year later.

1837 Aug 4   Voted at Lavenham for Logel and Rusbrook by order of Mr Stearn.

(Strangely, Mr Stearn was not William Scarfe's landlord, nor his boss. However, he was the principal resident landowner in Thorpe Morieux at the time and may have been able to exert pressure on William Scarfe, who was, at the age of 60, eligible to vote for the first time. This was not a secret ballot. Alternatively, 'by order of' may mean he was acting under the advice of Mr Stearn. He does use this expression more than once in this journal.)

1837 Aug 14   begun Harves at Hessett the Monday before felsham faire finished Harves at Hessett September 16 1837

Christian Name & Surname of each Voter.	Place of Abode.	Nature of Qualification.	Street, Lane, or other like Place in the Parish where the Property is situate or Name of the Property, or Name of the Tenant.
THORPE MORIEUX.			
7 Andrews John	Thorpe Morieux	Occupier of house and land	Near the Lavenham road
8 Aves Joseph	Thorpe Morieux	Freehold house	On the Bury road
9 Bigg Edward	Thorpe Morieux	Occupier of house and land	Near the Lavenham road
0 Edgar John	Thorpe Morieux	Occupier of land	On the Lavenham road
1 Goald Bixby [Thomas	Thorpe Morieux	Freehold house and land	Near the church
2 Harrison the Revd. Thomas	Thorpe Morieux	Freehold house and land	The rectory
3 Hustler Edward	Thorpe Morieux	Occupier of land	Near the Lavenham road
4 Last John	Thorpe Morieux	Occupier of house and land	Near the Bury road
5 Last James	Thorpe Morieux	Freehold house and land	Near the Bury road
6 Mumford Robert	Thorpe Morieux	Freehold house and land	Thorpe hall farm
7 Mudd Henry	Thorpe Morieux	Occupier of house and land	On the Bury road
8 Melton Frederick	Thorpe Morieux	Occupier of house and land	Near the Bury road
9 Melton Richard	Thorpe Morieux	Occupier of house and land	On the Bildeston road
0 North William	Thorpe Morieux	Freehold house and shop	Near the church
1 Newson William	Thorpe Morieux	Occupier of house and land	On the Bury road
2 Poynder Thomas	Clapham common	Freehold land	John Edgar and Robert Clarke, tenant
3 Payne Robert	Thorpe Morieux	Occupier of house and land	Near the Lavenham road
4 Roberts John	Thorpe Morieux	Freehold house and land	On the Lavenham road
5 Rush Samuel	Thorpe Morieux	Freehold house and land	Near the Lavenham road
6 Read Thomas	Grundisburgh	Freehold land	On the Bury road, Wm. Newson, tenant
7 Stearn John	Thorpe Morieux	Freehold land	On the Lavenham road
8 Smith Benjamin	Thorpe Morieux	Occupier of house and land	Near the Bury road
9 Stutley John	Clare	Freehold house and land	John Elder, tenant
0 Scott Thomas	Thorpe Morieux	Occupier of house and land	On the Bury road
1 Stearn Thomas	Thorpe Morieux	Freehold house and land	Near the Lavenham road
2 Scarpe William	Thorpe Morieux	Freehold house	On the Bury road
3 Scott John	Thorpe Morieux	Occupier of house and land	On the Bury road
4 Wilson John Maryon	Great Cranfield	Copyhold house and land	Benjamin Smith, tenant

Christian Name & Surname of each Voter.	Place of Abode.	Nature of Qualification.	Street, Lane, or other like Place in the Parish where the Property is situate, or Name of the Property, or Name of the Tenant.
FELSHAM ST. PETER.			
Anderson Thomas Revd. Rec-	Felsham	Freehold house and land	Rectory
Barnes John [tor	Buxhall, Suffolk	Freehold house and buildings	Near the green
Baker George	Felsham	Freehold house and land	Cockfield road
Boggiss James	Felsham	Occupier of house and land	On Bury road
Bletsoe Morgan John	Felsham	Freehold house and land	Brend's Hill farm
Cook James	Hyde Park corner	Freehold house and land	Felsham green
Cook Charles	Felsham	Freehold houses	Felsham green
Dalton William	Bury St. Edmund's	Freehold house and land	On the Gedding road
Dyer William	Felsham	Occupier of house and land	Brend's Hill farm
Hercy John	Bray, Berkshire	Freehold house and land	George Kerridge, tenant
Howe Francis	Felsham	Freehold house and buildings	Felsham green
Kerridge George	Felsham	Occupier of house and land	On the road to Gedding mill
Kinzey William	Felsham Bells inn	Occupier of house and land	Rands farm
Manfield William	Felsham	Occupier of house and land	Near Gedding mill
Melton Samuel	Felsham	Occupier of house and land	Brook hall
Nunn Thomas	Felsham	Occupier of house and land	Near the rectory
Roper Elijah	Felsham	Occupier of house and land	On road to Gedding mill
Sturgeon Isaac	Felsham	Freehold house and land	Slough farm
Steward William	Felsham	Occupier of house and land	Near Felsham hall
Watkinson George	Felsham	Occupier of house and land	Near the Slough farm

Poll Register for West Suffolk constituency, 1836

1837 Aug   In the month of August Mrs Resbrook hat her Leg Cut of

1837 Sep 16   finished in Sept 16th was very fine

1837 Oct 1   Settled with Wm Gladwell of Rattelsden

(John Gladwell is listed as a thatcher in Felsham in White's directory of 1844.)

1837 Oct 12   Bought the Glibe Grove of Mr Thos Anderson of felsham

(This seems to refer to a small finger of woodland in Felsham, known to this day as the Glebe Grove. Clearly, he was only securing a lease on this small area of woodland.)

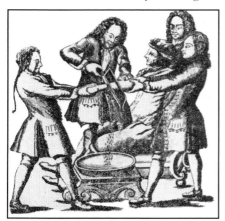

If pictures of amputations at the time are to be believed, such operations, without anaesthetic, must have been horrific.

1837 Oct 21   John Bird Died of Thorpe Green in Decline

*(Aged 40, he was buried at Thorpe on 27th October 1837.
This is not the same John Bird who was responsible for
two housekeepers becoming pregnant in October 1831. He
appears in the 1851 Census living in Brettenham.)*

1837 Nov 29   James Boggies wife Died of felsham farmer and
Dril man

*(May Bogges, aged 66, was buried at Felsham on 4th
December 1837.)*

1837   Mr Leehope was Bured the week be fore Crismiss
The Hole of the falmey Brought from London

*(Michael Peter Leheup, aged 55, was buried at Hessett on
20th December 1837. He was Lord of the Manor of Hessett
at the time of his death, and freeholder of the land farmed by
William's brother John.)*

1837   The same Day Mrs Leehope daughter was Bured
at Hessett

*(All a bit confusing, but this seems to refer to Marielena
Carpenter, buried at Hessett on 27th April 1837, aged just
26. The parish register for Hessett states that her body was
brought from London.)*

1837 Dec 21   Mr Stearns farmer of Thorpe had his corning
frollect was 3ds It was A very wit day

*(In the 1841 Census, John Stearn's address was given as
Thorpe Hill, now referred to as Hill Farm, to the south of
the village. This 'corning frolic' sounds like a kind of late
Harvest Horkey, though the fact it is on the shortest day may
be of significance. Alternatively, it could be a tithe feast,
another being mentioned in the journal on 10th December
1828.)*

1837 Dec 21   Lors our Meare Jipsy . . .

1837 Dec 28   Bought a Newen of Mr Hustler 12 0 0
               (This relates to the mare 'Gypsy' that died a week before.)

1837   In 1837 Fred Allington was at work at Livermeere
               (Might be written 'Livermoore'.)

1837   In 1837 George Howard got our sack is a farmer
               Brought it Hom

1837   Lizer Snell come to Thorpe from Bently

1838 Jan 5   Wm Sturgeon wife of Bradfield manyer Died
               (Aged 61, she was buried at Bradfield Combust.
               See also the entry for March 1842. 'The Manger'
               at Bradfield Combust is, at the time of writing, still
               a public house. It was a significant staging post for
               coaches. It is possible William Scarfe is referring not
               so much to the pub as to the village itself, calling the
               village 'Bradfield Manger'.)

1838 Jan 9   begun to snow It was very Could

1838 Jan 14   Hanner Offord was found Ded n her Bed given to
               have fits
               (Hannah Offord, aged 37, was buried at Thorpe on 21st
               January 1838.)

1838 Jan 27   Had our singing Frolick

1838 Jan 27   Thos Spark Died
               (Aged 80, he was buried at Thorpe on 2nd February 1838.)

1838 Jan   Had our singin Frolick that Mr Spark Died

Two early twentieth century postcards showing the road past William Scarfe's cottage and Thorpe Morieux Rectory.

1838 Jan 28   James Howard toke Mr North Grate Coat

1838 Jan   in Jan Lost a weeks work by the snow

1838 Jan In Janry Snow fell Lasted for a fortneth

1838 the frost was very Sharpe for a forneth Whe Lost 3 weeks

1838 Feb 6 Miss Harot Stearn marred to C Scott

(Charles Scott and Harriett Stearn were both farmers of Thorpe.)

1838 Feb 28 Rob Pilbrow Died of Kittelson son of Wm Pilbrow of felsham Clarke

(This date may be wrong. He was not buried at Kettlebaston. One Robert Pilbrow, aged 24, was buried at Felsham on 10th May 1844; another by the same name, aged 43, was buried at St James, Bury St Edmunds, on 13th June 1843. Though not an uncommon name, it may be significant that a Robert Pilbrow was named in 1839 as the putative father of a male bastard child born to Mary Anne Lyes of Barrow.)

1838 Feb It begun to thow on Feb 24 the Snow Lasted for 7 weeks

1838 Feb Thomas North Died

(He was buried Feb 4th at Thorpe aged 82.)

1838 Mar 11 Mrs Chinery Came to our House from Rattelsden old Mrs Scarfe was taken very Ill the same times

1838 Mar 16 Thos Sparkes Sale at Thorpe Moriuex

(About six weeks after he had died at the singing frolic.)

1838 Apr 6 John Long Die on the 6 at Bulles wood

(Aged 50, he was buried at Thorpe on 11th April 1838. He had once been a labourer working with William Scarfe.)

1838 Apr 7   Mr Hustler Died of Thorpe farmer
              (Charles Edward Hustler, aged 41, buried at Thorpe on 14th
              April 1838.)

1838 Apr 10   James Boggis Died of felsham farmer
              (Aged 64, he was buried at Felsham on 16th April 1838.)

1838 Apr 15   young Plumb of Rattelsden fell Down Brook his neck
              (John Plume, aged 48, was buried at Rattlesden on 20th
              April 1838.)

1838 Apr 16   *(James Boggis)* attended by the Felsham Club 51
              members folled him to the Church

1838 Apr 18   John Estling at Bilderstone Died in Decline the
              felsham Club atended the funel
              (John Esling, aged 32, was buried at Bildeston on 23rd April
              1838.)

1838 May 2   finished Brushing in felsham wood the weather
              was very could

1838 May 17   Master Noah was kild at Samer Hill by a wagen
              (This may be Semer Hill, a major hazard on the road to
              Hadleigh.)

1838 May   begun to Peeling Bark in Thorpe wood 1838 Wm
              Scarfe Ed Crick John Long Elfred Goold in May

1838   Had Tom Crick 3 weeks 16 6 Helping whe in
              Thorpe Wood
              (He was Edward Crick's 17 year old son.)

1838 May 24   finished Barke peling Thorpe Wood A fortenith
              and 3 days half come at 12 shillings a week

The danger on the roads

Unfortunately, Coroners' records for West Suffolk in the mid-nineteenth century have been lost. However, inquest reports on sudden deaths for coastal areas of the county would indicate that about 15% of all sudden deaths involved vehicles. Travelling on carts, wagons and tumbrels was a dangerous business. There are several court cases, reported at the time, of people being indicted for the dangerous practice of riding on the shafts of wagons.

1838 May   in May Joel Raker hurt himself he fell of a hose Going Home

1838 Jun 23   had a swam of Bees frances heved them be Long to Mrs Scarfe

1838 Jun 24   Bought of George Howard a pig 16s

1838 Jul 24   Richd Offord was Publish to Eley
(On 1st July 1838, Richard Offord, labourer, married Mary Ann Eley at Thorpe.)

1838 Jun 27   had a festble at Thorpe on the count of the Squire
(This is the only reference to the village's celebration of Queen Victoria's Coronation, which was attended by the whole Scarfe family.)

A most remarkable survival from this time is a portion of a notebook in which Mr Stearn wrote his plans for this celebration. According to this, nine tickets were allotted to 'Scarff'. This would presumably have been William Scarfe and wife, his son and wife and their five children.

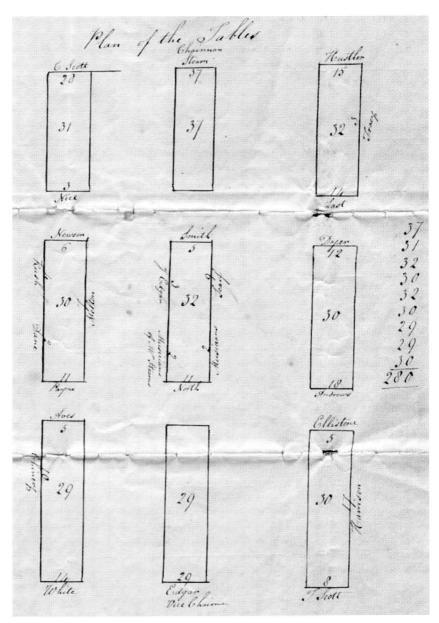

The people of Thorpe enjoyed a day of feasting and fun – here is a seating plan for 280 people sitting down to dinner – whilst three miles away in Lavenham virtually nothing was done by way of celebration.

Toasts

1. Her most Gracious Majesty Queen Victoria long may she reign
2. Her Majesty the Queen Dowager
3. Her Royal Highness the Duchess of Kent
4. His Royal Highness the ~~Duchess~~ Duke of Sussex
5. Success to Agriculture and Trade
6. Success to the Parish of Thorpe
7. The Peasantry of England
8. The Chairman
9. The Ladies

The following was inserted in the Bury Post

At Thorpe Morieux on Thursday the Labourers and Families amounting to 300 partook of an excellent dinner in celebration of the Coronation provided by their respective Masters in a meadow of Mr J Stearn who presided on the occasion after appropriate toasts where drunk rural sports commenced an continued till 6 o'clock when the party adjourned to a convenient building and partook of tea and plum cake and excellent band being in attendance the merry dance was kept up till 11 O'clock when they retired to their homes next morning they reassembled and partook of the fragments and remaining portion of beer which was equally distributed they then returned peaceably to their homes with every feeling of gratitude for their bountiful feast.

Memorandum ½ lb of meat ⅜ lb of bread and 1 quart of beer for head taking little and great would have been sufficient for a good frolick

Although the Bury Post *was overwhelmed with reports of similar village celebrations it still found space to print Mr Stearn's description of what happened at Thorpe Morieux. A transcript of the Thorpe report as it appeared in the* Bury Post, *alongside a report for Lavenham, appears in* Newspapers in Suffolk *vol. 3 by P. and J. Wright.*

1838 Jun 28   Wm Scarfe when to Hessett

1838 Jul 4   Wm Pilbrow Died Clarke of felsham Parish be
Long to the felsham Club
*(Thomas William Pilbrow, aged 77, was buried at Felsham
on 8th July 1838.)*

1838 Jul 28   The Confomation *(confirmation)* was at Bilderstone
the young popel whent from Thorpe Morriuex

1838 Jul 29   Whent to Bayton

1838 Aug   begun Harves in Aug at Hessett
*(This refers to William helping his brother John with the
harvest as he did other years.)*

1838 Aug 19   Lavenham singins when to felsham Church the
Sunday After the Fair young Mr Rushbrock
Thorpe singins when with them to felsham

1838 Nov   in Nov had 3 New winders frames in our house by
Mr North 1 11 0

1838 Dec 12   Mrs Lister Drownded her self at felsham
*(Susan Lister, aged 68, was buried at Felsham on 13th
December 1838.)*

1838 Dec 15   Charles White Died at Brettenham Left his son
Charles some very Hamsum
*(White, aged 80, was buried at Brettenham on 21st
December 1838.)*

1838 Dec 16   Edw Crick named his Child his name is George
This Make 15 Childen

1838   Arnilia *(Amelia?)* Estling Died at London

1839 Jan 1 Good Deel of Snow fell the first Day of Janry

1839 Jan 6 Mrs Lane of felsham was Burnt to Ded the wife of
Rob Lane

*(Susan Lane, aged 78, was buried at Felsham on 10th
February 1838.)*

1839 Jan 6 Mrs Scotts child very Ill

1839 Jan 8 had a Singing frolick at John Howards of Thorpe I
Left of Singing with them

1839 Jan 9 Wm Scarfe Bought a New Grate Coate at Bury
and A New Hat of Mr Hym Coate and Hat 1 12 0

*(It was time for William Scarfe to visit Mr Hyam again; see
the entry for 17th October 1828.)*

L. HYAM,

TAILOR, WOOLLEN DRAPER, AND HATTER,

BUTTER MARKET, BURY ST. EDMUND'S,

(OPPOSITE THE BANK OF MESSRS. OAKES AND CO.

BEGS to call the attention of his numerous Friends and the Public to the under-mentioned List of Prices, FOR ARTICLES MADE TO ORDER. Having made extensive purchases on the most advantageous terms (for Cash), and every Article being cut on the premises, and made under his own superintendence in the best possible style, he is determined that no effort shall be wanting to render this Establishment a real benefit to his customers. From those who have not yet availed themselves of the above advantages, he begs an early call, confident that those who purchase once are certain of coming again, every Article being of GOOD QUALITY, and Sold at the

LOWEST REMUNERATING PROFIT.

Every description of Ready-made Clothes in great variety, an immense Stock of GREAT COATS of the most fashionable materials.

PILOT GREAT COAT, Velvet Collar, lined with Check, 15s.
PETERSHAM Ditto, 21s.; SUPERFINE SURTOUT and DRESS COATS, from 30s.;
CLOTH FROCKS, from 26s.; SHOOTING COAT, from 12s.;
CASSIMERE BREECHES, from 15s.; CORD Ditto, from 5s.;
Striped Buckskin Trousers, from 11s.; Beaverteen, Cord, Check, and Cantoon ditto, from 4s. 6d.;
Cloth Waistcoats, from 6s.; Double-breasted do., 8s. 6d.; Valencia do., from 4s. 6d.; Check do., 3s.;

BOYS' AND YOUTHS' CLOTHES EQUALLY CHEAP.

MOURNING OF EVERY DESCRIPTION KEPT READY MADE.

OBSERVE.—*No Business done at this Establishment from Sunset on Friday until Saturday Evening, after which it will be opened for Business until Eleven o'clock.*

L. HYAM's List of Prices for Gentlemen's Clothes, made to order, in the most Fashionable and Elegant Style:—

COATS.	£. s. d.	BREECHES.	£. s. d.
Gentlemen's fine Dress Coats	1 14 0	Cassimere	0 16 0
Saxony ditto	2 2 0	Ditto, best manufactured	1 1 0
Imperial ditto	2 8 0	Cotton Cord ditto, from	0 8 0
Extra ditto, the best Manufactured	2 12 6	Woollen ditto, from	0 13 0
Superfine Surtout Coat, silk facings	1 18 0	Cassimere Gaiters, from	0 7 0
Imperial ditto	2 8 0		
Extra ditto, the very best	2 18 0	WAISTCOATS.	
Beaverteen or Cantoon Shooting Coats,		Summer Waistcoats, new patterns,	
from	0 18 0	7s. each, or 3 for	1 0 0
Velveteen ditto	1 1 0	Silk Valencia ditto	

1839 Jan 11   Mrs Scarfe was taken very Ill with a Bad Could

1839 Jan 26   Elizabeth Allington Left Miss Youngs of Bradfield Manger Lived with Her A good meny yeares John Allington Kept her Company
(See the entry for 26th February 1839.)

1839 Jan 28   Mrs North of Thorpe was Confined with A Gall the wife of Wm North Carpenter
(The child's name was Mary Ann, named after her mother.)

1839 Feb 10   George Blumfield Died
(Aged 17, buried at Thorpe on 17th February 1839.)

1839 Feb 12   Isac Spite was robed at Lavenham faire

(Fairs were notorious places for pickpockets and thieves. Whilst we were unable to find a report of this particular crime, newspapers of the time recount a theft of £245 at Lavenham Fair from Mr Lansdell. Three likely rogues were arrested, by the names of Wythe, Woods and Cullum, but they were able to show they had attended the fair to sell their wares and were acquitted, in spite of having been in possession of some of the missing notes.)

1839 Feb 15   Fraces Scarfe was Confind
(The second wife of his son William Scarfe Jnr did not have her only child of this union until a year later. It seems likely she had a stillbirth which was never baptised and remains unrecorded.)

1839 Feb 18   it snowed all the Day Long

1839 Feb 26   Eizabeth Allington was marred to John Allington of Bradfield Manger Lived a Long with Miss youngs at Bradfield Magner Lived with her a good meney yeares

(Elizabeth Alderton, daughter of Simon Alderton, married Robert Alderton son of John Alderton at Bradfield Combust. Robert was the blacksmith at Little Whelnetham. Yet again, the parish of Bradfield Combust is being referred to by the name of the coaching inn that still trades there today.)

1839 Feb

in Feb John Langham of Cockfield his man got hurt by the wageon by the Name of Sowgate he Los his Life

(Robert Southgate, aged 35, was buried at Cockfield on 24th February 1839. His inquest was reported in the Suffolk Herald.)

INQUEST.—By Harry Wayman Gent, Coroner for the Liberty and Borough of Bury St. Edmund's.—At Cockfield, on Thursday last, on the body of Robert Southgate, who was killed by falling accidentally under the wheel of a waggon. It appeared from the evidence of George Cockridge, that on Monday, last about four in the afternoon, as he and deceased were returning from Stowmarket with a waggon laden with coals ; that he went to turn the leader of the horses on the road, and on turning round, heard the deceased cry out " George ;" then saw him under the wheel, which was between his legs, with his hands clasping the shafts ; he was forced along in this way 7 or 8 yards ; he had previously been riding on the shafts ; the accident must have been occasioned by his attempting to get off them ; the deceased was between 30 and 40 years of age.—Verdict, " Accidental Death."

1839 Mar 7

it snowed all the Day Long It was a very Could Day

(The Southwold diary of James Maggs describes 'heavy falls of snow, March 6th & 7th'.)

1839 Mar 14

It Rayned A good Deel the wind was Could

(Dated 14th and 15th March.)

1839 Mar 23

John Cagg of Brettenham Died in A fit ben out with a wageon

> ———On the 25th
> inst. in the parish of Brettenham, on the body of John
> Cadge. Joseph Bramford deposed, that he assisted
> deceased on Saturday morning in loading a quantity of
> faggots; after having done which he proceeded forward
> to to a beer house for the purpose of getting some re-
> freshment ready for deceased by the time he came up.
> Witness offered Cadge some bread, which he refused, he
> then offered beer to him, which he put to his lips and
> returned the mug without swallowing any, saying " it
> appeared like poison to him." This witness took to be
> indicative of illness on the part of deceased, he being
> very fond of beer. Witness stopped at another beer-
> shop, however, to get some more beer, when the deceased
> partook of a small quantity with him. When they were
> unloading the waggon at witness's house he saw de-
> ceased gently sliding from the waggon, and upon getting
> him into the house, and placing him on a chair, life was
> found to be extinct. He was between 60 and 70 years
> of age. Verdict—Died in a fit of apoplexy by the visi-
> tation of God.

(John Cadge, aged 70, was buried at Brettenham on 27th March 1839. His inquest was reported in the Suffok Herald. *What is not clear is whether the faggots he was carting came from William Scarfe at Thorpe.)*

1839 Mar 24   Mager Harrison is very Ill

1839 Apr 17   finish Brushing In Thorpe wood for Mr Jossylen

1839 Apr   the weather was very Wet and could for time yeare

1839 May 6   be gun to Peel Barke in Thorpe Wood Wm Scarfe
Edw Crick John Bird Wm Lister

1839 May 13   *(John Cadge – see entry for 23rd March 1839)* his wife
marred May 13 to young Osborn of Brettenham
(now) had husBand *(husband)*
(John Osborn, labourer, married Sarah Cadge, widow.)

1839 May 14   had a good Deel of Snow it was very Could

1839 Jun 14   Mr T Harrison son Died at Briton School Brught Home

(Ralph Ward Harrison, aged 9, was buried at Thorpe on 21st June 1839.)

1839 Jul 19   Mager Harrison come to Brook Hall felsham from Copford Hall Essex

1839 Jul 21   Wm Rush Marrided to Sarah Palmer

Copford Hall, near Colchester, the home of the Harrison family.

(He was the son of the Thorpe blacksmith. They appear as husband and wife in the 1851 census for Thorpe under the name Rust. At their marriage, he was 19, she was just 20. Very few seem to have married as young as this in this area.)

1839 Dec 11   Mager Harrison of Copford Hall was Buryed at Thorpe Died at London Aged 84 Mr S Cral Made sermon

(John Haynes Harrison – aged 83 in the parish register.)

1839   in 1839 the flower was three shillings per stone

1839   Tomes Goold was very Ill in Decline could not work his mother Died in Decline

1839   Tomes Goold was very Ill not Like to Recover

(This appears as two entries which are probably referring to the same person. Whether it is James or Thomas is unclear. Either way, he appears to have recovered: no Goold burials were found for this period and he sang at Hessett with William Scarfe in July 1840 – see the entry for 19th July 1840.)

1839   The Bark Run very Bad Wm Scarfe Edw Crick John Crick John Bird Wm Lister

1840 Jan 15   Frances Scarfe was Confind with a Gall The wife of Wm Scarfe Jn of Thorpe

('Baptised to William (woodman) & Frances, a daughter, Mary, February 20th 1840.')

1840 Jan   In Janry had ower New oven meade by John

Nethergates of Cockfield	his Bill 16s 0d
for lime and Brick	15s 10d
Nethergates Bill	16s 0d
(total)	1 11 10

1840 Mar 24   Hezekier Harrison was Bured in Thorpe Church
yard Died at Barlfield *(Little Bardfield, Essex)* Rector
of Thorpe

*(He was 79 and had been Rector of Thorpe Morieux from
1786 to 1823.)*

the old Mager Harrison Died in December 1839

1840 Jun 7   Mrs Haselood Died at Gedding Suffolk Left 4
Children

*(Matilda Haselwood, aged 28, was buried at Gedding on
11th June 1840.)*

1840 Jul 11   Entred our House in to the Thorpe Coat Roles
(Court Rolls) paid 8s 10d Mr James Subbings
Stward of the Coat

The Manor Court of Thorpe Morieux

*The ledgers containing minutes and proceedings of the court
are still available to view at Bury St Edmunds Record Office.
For the fee of one shilling a year, William Scarfe Senior
was able to register his freehold tenure of the cottage that
served as two dwellings. We are also told that the previous
occupants of the house had been Edward Stearne and John
Mumford. The departure of Mumford had enabled William
Scarfe Junior to occupy the other end of his father's house.
All this had only been possible, of course, by virtue of John
Scarfe's generosity.*

1840 Jul 19   Wm Scarfe Tomes Goold whent to Hessett Church
to Sing

1840 Jul 27   finish ting up lits In Thorpe wood

*('Tying up lits' may refer to bundles of litter or lights,
meaning faggots for bread ovens)*

The earliest known picture of Moat Farm Cottage, home of the Scarfe family for over 80 years. The people pictured are Scarfes around the beginning of the twentieth century.

1840 Jul — In the month of July James Coopers wife Died he be Long to the felsham Club

1840 Aug — begun Harvest at Hessett

1840 Aug 15 — had 2 New gates meade by Mr North

1840 Aug 16 — Mr John Scarfe was come to felsham fair

1841 Feb 18 — Charles Snell Died at Thorpe

(Aged 65, he was buried at Thorpe on 23rd February 1841.)

1841 Feb 21 — John Tweed was Bured at Bradfield 57 members at his funel

(Tweed, aged 74, was buried at Bradfield St George on 21st February 1841.)

These were the homes of two of William Scarfe's closest neighbours,
John Palmer (above) and William North (below).
William North's cottage is still called 'Wheelwrights'.

1841 Apr 10   finished Brushing in thorpe wood

1841 Dec 23   John Howards Died of thorpe
(John Howard, aged 69, was buried at Thorpe on 30th December 1841.)

1842 Mar 13   Thos Smith Wm Sturgeon was Bured at Bradfield manger
(They were both buried that day at Bradfield Combust. Thomas Smith was 53, William Sturgeon was 75.)

1842 Jun 7   John Scarfe had his Lip sowing up by Mr Grouse of Bilderstone

1842 Sep 29   Henery Mudd Died Thorpe
(Henry Mudd, aged 71, was buried at Thorpe on 4th October 1842.)

1842   Wm Scarfe Lost his sterngth
(Whatever he suffered at this point, his output in the journal is much reduced from now on.)

1843 Jan 23   the wife of Wm North Died
(Mary Ann Sarah North, aged 43, was buried at Thorpe on 28th January 1843.)

1843 Mar 2   Call on the Club

1843 Apr   in April Susan Steff Died Bured the 2 of May at Preston
(Susan Stiff, aged 62.)

1843 Jun 25   in June John Palmer wife Died Bured June 25 at Thorpe
(Maria Palmer, aged 35)

1843 Jun   Robert Grimwood marred to Susan Howard of
            Thorpe
            *(They were both listed as labourers and married at Thorpe
            on 11th June.)*

1844 Jan 16 Lueaser Raker Marrid to Hen Spink of Bayton
            *(The banns for Beyton in January 1844 name them as Henry
            Spink of Beyton and Louisa Raker of Brettenham. He was a
            wheelwright, she was a farmer's daughter. They married at
            Brettenham.)*

1844 Jun 24 Wm Scarfe Se *(senior)* Mist Going to the Club
            Feast at felsham Bells

1845 Feb 16 Isaac Orsborn was Bured at Cockfield 60
            Members attended his funel
            (Aged 67, he was buried at Cockfield on 17th February 1845.)

1845 Mar 15 Edw Howlett Died at Bayton
            (Aged 57, he was buried that day at Beyton.)

1845 Jun 30 Fredrick Allngton com to thorpe

1845 Jul 9   Jams Makings got hurt by a Wageon Mr Marshall
            of Felsham

1845 Jul   John Arnhold Died
            *(John Arnold, aged 33, was buried at Hessett on 2nd August
            1845.)*

1846 Apr 19 Samuel Brinkley Died
            (He was buried, aged 64, on 24th April at Thorpe.)

1847 Jan   John Estling Died at felsham
            (He was buried at Felsham on 29th January, aged 64.)

After this entry there are no more entries for 15 pages. The rest seem to be written by a different hand.

1847 Feb 9   John Scarfe of Hessett died Bured at Bayton
               (The brother of William Scarfe senior, aged 83, was buried at Beyton on 16th February 1847.)

1848 Aug   William Scarfe Sener Died AugeTs 1848
               (The author of most of this journal, aged 70, was buried at Thorpe on 6th August 1848. His Death Certificate records an incorrect age of 67. His daughter-in-law, Frances Scarfe, registered his death. The cause was given as 'exhaustion from Diarrhoea 5 months Certified'. Modern medical advice suggests he may have had cancer of the colon.)

1849 Nov 19   Old Master Raffe Died Aged 91
               (This might be 1843.)

1850 Nov 5   Mises Scarfe Thorpe Died
               (Mary Scarfe, widow of William Scarfe senior, aged 78, was buried at Thorpe on 10th November 1850.)

1855 Apr 13   Susener Scarfe wife of Esau Scarfe was Confind with a gall
               (They baptised a daughter, Elizabeth Scarff, at Thorpe on 27th May 1855. She was the first of their six children. Esau was described in the parish register as a farmer.)

HC 744725

CERTIFIED COPY of an
Pursuant to the Births and

ENTRY OF DEATH
Deaths Registration Act 1953

Registration District   Cosford

1848.   Death in the Sub-district of   Lavenham   in the   County   of   Suffolk

No.	When and where died	Name and surname	Sex	Age	Occupation	Cause of death	Signature, description, and residence of informant	When registered	Signature of registrar
Columns: -	1	2	3	4	5	6	7	8	9
268	First August 1848 Thorpe	William SCARFE	Male	68 years	Woodman	Exhaustion from Diarrhoea 5 months Certified.	The mark of X Frances Scarfe present at death Thorpe	Fourth August 1848	Geo Scott Registrar.

'Certified to be a true copy of an entry in a register in my custody.

_____ Deputy Superintendent Registrar

27th September 2001   Date

CAUTION: THERE ARE OFFENCES RELATING TO FALSIFYING OR ALTERING A CERTIFICATE AND USING OR POSSESSING A FALSE CERTIFICATE ®CROWN COPYRIGHT

WARNING: A CERTIFICATE IS NOT EVIDENCE OF IDENTITY.

A modern copy of the death certificate for William Scarfe

Undated entries

Only a small number of entries are undated. Most of those can be worked out. The following entries, however, could not be placed with any certainty.

Apr 21   John Goold of Felsham was taken very Ill

Oct 20   Mr Langham came to our House from Cockfield

The virgin Mary was Churched on Candlemas Day after Christ was Boarn

Jan 2   Wm Scarfe S Ented in to the Felsham Club

Wm Scarfe S served as under Clark in the felsham Club for a yeare

---

Self-help clubs and their rules

William Scarfe first mentions the Felsham Club in 1827, but not until 1830 does he really indicate his own membership (see the detail with January 1830 entries). Not until 1833 does he give a description of his involvement in their financial management. Though the Felsham Club has proved elusive, Ipswich Record Office has a copy of the rules relating to Brundish Friendly Society dated 1838 which may have operated in much the same way. Members took it in turns to serve as officers of the club. It seems likely William Scarfe had belonged to the Felsham Club for some time as his age would almost certainly have made him ineligible for entry to the club above the age of fifty.

A sample of practice items from the book

There are any number of these in the Prayer Book. Some are clearly copied from the page they occupy. Others are endless repeats of the first item shown here. Sometimes lists of numbers are part of the practice. Other entries are biblical texts and rhymes such as one might find in an autograph book.

William Scarfe his Book May 14 1827
The Gift of Mr Tomes Harrison Rector of Thorpe
Parish in County of Suffolk

Of the 47 pslam 7 vers
god is king of All the Earth
Blessed is the man feare the Lord

William Scarfe his book The gift of the
revent Tommes Harrison Recter of Thorpe
Morriuex In the year of our Lord 1828

Edward Elsden of Bradfield
(Written three times in succession with no further detail)

god meade man and man meade money
god meade Bees and Bees mede Honey

Blessed is the man that Theareth the Lord
Blessed is the man Fearth the Lord for in the
hands of the Lord theare is a cup and the
wine is Red   May 1827

Mary Scarfe Her Book April 18 1827 Thorpe

The 47 psalm 7 vers God is king of All
the Earth Sing ye pray of understanding
Wrote April 18 1827

god save the King Happay is the man that fined
Wisdom A Covetous man is Never Satisfied
May 27 1827

William Scarfe His Book March 18 1827
The Gift of Thoms Harison To be given to John
Scarfe After my Death

*(By this, he may have meant his brother, but that John Scarfe
was 13 years his senior. Perhaps he meant his grandson to
receive the book. It is believed that John Scarfe, grandson to
William Scarfe senior, did indeed become the next keeper of
the Prayer Book as it passed down through his line.)*

Steal not This Book for fear the Shame
for Heare you se the owners Name
When This you se Rember me
And keepe me In your Mind
Let all The World Say what Thay will
Spake of me as you find

From the Journal of William Scarfe
(dated 1828)

Family history details

Here we see typical family Prayer Book or Family Bible entries, mostly written on the end cover. We can tell they were added at a later date as many of the dates precede the book's publication.

1772 Mar 25   Mary Scarfe *(formerly Mary Allington or Alderton)* was Boarn March 25 1772

1777 Oct 22   Wm Scarfe was Born at Felsham October 22 1777
(There is also an entry that dates his birth as 28th September. Acording to the Felsham parish register, he was baptised on 19th October 1777, so clearly the date above is wrong.)

1764   His Brother John was Born in the year of 1764 at Bradfield St George
(November 10th – the journal mentions celebrating his birthday in 1832.)

The Settlement of William Scarfe's parents

Any family living and working outside their own parish could be forcibly moved back by way of a legal removal order, if the overseers of their temporary place of settlement believed they might require poor relief. In 1783, before William Scarfe was born, his parents along with elder brother John and sister Elizabeth, were moved from Bradfield St George, back to Felsham. We know this because the removal order and the settlement order, drawn up between the two parishes, both survive in the County archives. Four years later, John and Elizabeth Scarfe baptised their son, William Scarfe, in Felsham.

(No. 38.)

R. B.

2777/2/35

Suffolk, to wit:

To the Church-Wardens and Overseers of the Poor of the Parish ------ of Bradfield Saint George ---- in the said County --- and to the Church-Wardens and Overseers of --- the Poor of the Parish --- of Felsham --- in the said County. ---

------ and to each and every of them

UPON the Complaint of the Church-Wardens and Overseers of the Poor of the Parish --- ------ --- of Bradfield George in the County --- --- of Suffolk --- unto us whose Names are hereunto set and Seals affixed, being two of his Majesty's Justices of the Peace in and for the said County --- of Suffolk and one of us of the Quorum, that John Scarfe and Elizabeth his wife, and John their Son aged about --- Eight years, and Elizabeth their Daughter aged about four years --- --- ---

did lately come to inhabit in the said Parish of Bradfield Saint George --- not having gained a legal Settlement there, nor produced any Certificate owning them --- to be settled elsewhere, and that the said John Scarfe and Elizabeth his wife and John and Elizabeth their Children are --- --- ---

--- --- --- likely to be chargeable to the said Parish --- of Bradfield Saint George We the said Justices upon due Proof made thereof, as well upon the Examination of the said John Scarfe --- upon Oath, as otherwise, and likewise upon due Consideration had of the Premises, do adjudge the same to be true; and we do likewise adjudge, that the lawful Settlement of them the said John Scarfe and Elizabeth his wife and John and Elizabeth their Children --- ---

is in the said Parish --- of Felsham --- in the said County --- of Suffolk --- We do therefore require you the said Church-Wardens and Overseers of the Poor of the said Parish --- --- of Bradfield Saint George or some, or one of you, to convey the said John Scarfe and Elizabeth his wife and John and Elizabeth their Children ---

from and out of your said Parish of Bradfield Saint George to the said Parish of Felsham --- and them to deliver to the Church-Wardens and Overseers of the Poor there, or to some, or one of them, together with this our Order, or a true Copy thereof: And we do also hereby require you the said Church-Wardens and Overseers of the Poor of the said Parish of Felsham, to receive and provide for them ------ as Inhabitants of your said Parish. Given under our Hands and Seals the Seventh Day of July ------ in the Year of our Lord One Thousand Seven Hundred and Twenty three,

John Godbold

C. Metcalfe

The Removal Order for 1773,
removing the parents of William Scarfe from Bradfield St George to Felsham

1804 Dec 25   Wm Scarfe Jn was Boarn at Bradfield St Clare
December 25 18*(0)*4

1812 Jan 13   Elizabeth Scarfe of felsham Died Age 70 was
Bured at Felsham

(She was the mother of William Scarfe Senior.)

1814 Sep 14   Elizabeth Allington Died Sptem 14 1814 Aeged 72
was Bured at Bradfield St Clare Died at Bayton

*(She was the mother of Mary Scarfe, William Scarfe Senior's
wife.)*

1824 Dec 3   Mytilda Scarfe Died In the 18 year of age was
Bured at Felsham

(She was the daughter of William Scarfe Senior.)

1826 Mar 10   John Scarfe was Boarn at Thorpe March 10 1826
Son of Myrier Scarfe Maria Bogges felsham
Green farmer and Drilman

*(The eldest son of William Scarfe Junior, and a later keeper
of the Prayer Book.)*

1826 Nov 19   John Scarfe Died at Thorpe Moriuex Aged 85 was
Bured at Felsham

*(He was the father of William Scarfe Senior and John
Scarfe of Hessett.)*

Appendices

The Scarfe family

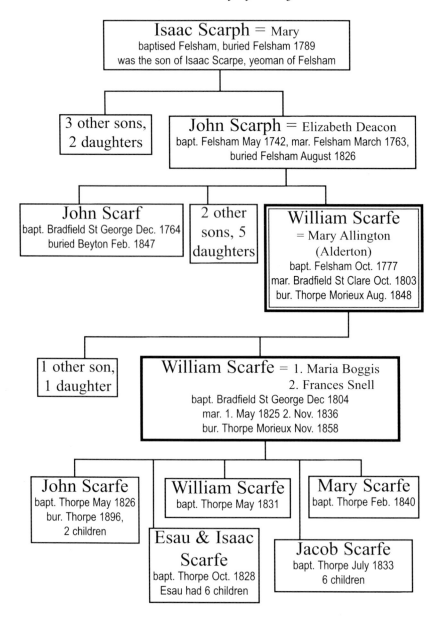

Isaac Scarph = Mary
baptised Felsham, buried Felsham 1789
was the son of Isaac Scarpe, yeoman of Felsham

3 other sons,
2 daughters

John Scarph = Elizabeth Deacon
bapt. Felsham May 1742, mar. Felsham March 1763,
buried Felsham August 1826

John Scarf
bapt. Bradfield St George Dec. 1764
buried Beyton Feb. 1847

2 other
sons, 5
daughters

William Scarfe
= Mary Allington
(Alderton)
bapt. Felsham Oct. 1777
mar. Bradfield St Clare Oct. 1803
bur. Thorpe Morieux Aug. 1848

1 other son,
1 daughter

William Scarfe = 1. Maria Boggis
2. Frances Snell
bapt. Bradfield St George Dec 1804
mar. 1. May 1825 2. Nov. 1836
bur. Thorpe Morieux Nov. 1858

John Scarfe
bapt. Thorpe May 1826
bur. Thorpe 1896,
2 children

William Scarfe
bapt. Thorpe May 1831

Mary Scarfe
bapt. Thorpe Feb. 1840

Esau & Isaac Scarfe
bapt. Thorpe Oct. 1828
Esau had 6 children

Jacob Scarfe
bapt. Thorpe July 1833
6 children

The Scarfe family in Felsham

THE EARLIEST RECORD OF A SCARFE in Felsham comes in 1460 when a feoffment describes land adjacent to property late of Walter Scarpe. There are several other entries through all the centuries leading up to the writing of the Prayer Book journal.

Though the spellings change, and it is difficult to produce an unbroken line, the family seems to have been present throughout most of four centuries. The family must once have been rather better off, as some are referred to as 'yeomen'; one is even described as a 'gentleman'. Some of the most interesting details describe the end of the life of William Scarfe's grandfather, Isaac, who appears to have fallen on hard times. In 1780, when he was already an old man, the Overseers' book for Felsham records him living in a parish house, paying 3s 6d a week rent. This seems to alter with his circumstances: over the following seven years, his rent fluctuates between 2s and 4s a week. He is listed as receiving poor relief of one shilling in 1787. Clearly unwell, he was cared for by Widow Pratt, who was paid by the parish to look after him. He seems to have recovered. Then in 1789, after a period of reduced rent payments, the following entries appear in the Parish Accounts:

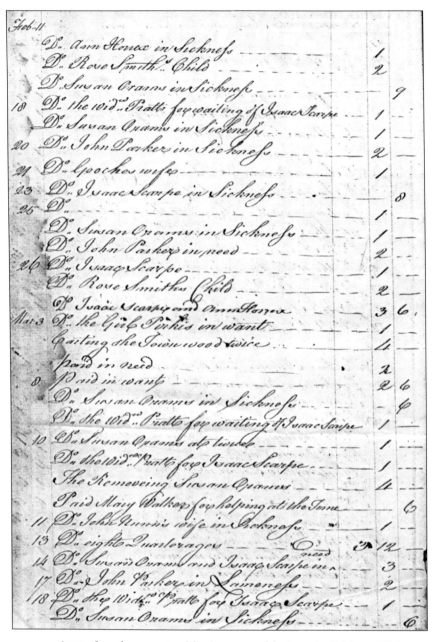

A page from the accounts of the Overseers of the Poor for Felsham, 1787

Paid for laying forth of old Scarpe	2 - 6
Paid to John Chapman for the bell	
& graves for 3 parish burials	8 - 6
Paid for the bearers for carrying old Scarpe	4 - 0
Deeks for shaving old Scarpe	2 - 6
Wm. Smith for Town coffins	18 - 6

'Woodcutters resting' by A. J. Stark

The Rectors of Thorpe Morieux

THE THORPE MORIEUX that William Scarfe knew would have been dominated by a handful of powerful families. The Harrisons of Copford Hall in Essex owned much of the surrounding land as well as commanding the living of Thorpe. Three Harrisons occupied the parsonage during the nineteenth century. The Sparrows, who were Lords of the Manor in William Scarfe's time, and the Fiskes were both linked to the Harrisons through marriage.

Rectors of the parish

1701 Joseph Sparrow
1719 John Fiske
1754 John Fiske Jnr
1778 Peter Edge
1781 John Sparrow
1786 Hezekiah Goodeve Harrison
1823 Thomas Thomas Harrison
1868 William Thomas Harrison
1875 Robert Charles Temple
1899 Frank Hamilton Cahusac
1903 William Thomas Harrison

The family tree of Rev. Thomas Thomas Harrison

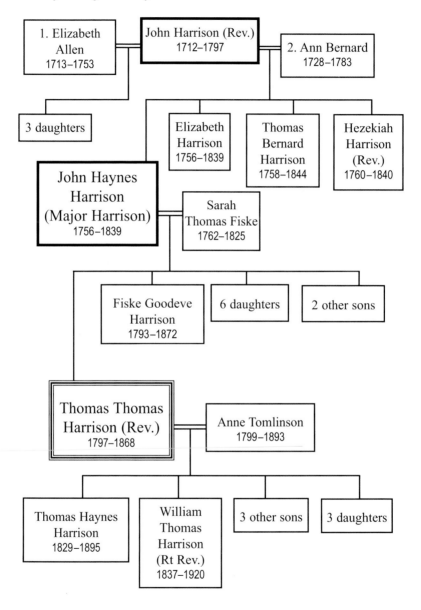

The Harrison family are well represented by monuments in and around Thorpe Morieux church. Thomas Thomas Harrison, who presented the prayer book to William Scarfe, has a substantial monument on the northern side of the church. This is a little bit of a mystery, as the North side was generally regarded as the least favoured and a Rector of forty-five years standing might have been expecting a plot to the south or east, if not inside the church itself. However, today's churchwardens have suggested the Southern aspect may have been waterlogged in years past, whereas it has always been drier to the north of Thorpe church.

Thomas Thomas Harrison and his wife appear to have been fondly remembered. An early church guide pamphlet describes him as a quiet, reserved man whose vivacious wife more than compensated for his shyness. As a couple they are described as being friendly and hospitable.

Inside St Mary's church, Thorpe, the great East window above the altar bears the names of Thomas Thomas Harrison and his family and serves as their lasting memorial.

Thomas Thomas Harrison's tomb on the north side of Thorpe church.

The East window of Thorpe Morieux church

William Thomas Harrison, the
second surviving son of Thomas
Thomas Harrison, was the
last of the Harrison rectors.
After ministering in Thorpe, he
became Bishop of Glasgow; he
then returned to Thorpe for a
second period as Rector; he was
regarded as an honorary Bishop
of Ely.

Rev. Thomas
Thomas Harrison gave
this prayer book to a
parishioner whom he
knew to be extremely
poor yet able to read
and write. We can
imagine him trying
to encourage William
Scarfe in his literacy
as well as in leading a
godly life.

Prayer on entering Church.

ASSIST us, Lord, in these our prayers and supplications; and grant that
those things which we ask faithfully, we may obtain effectually, through Jesus
Christ our Lord.

When the Service is ended.

THANKS be to thy holy Name, most gracious God, for this opportunity
of attending thy public service; and grant, O Lord, that neither our inattention
or want of devotion may render our imperfect petitions unacceptable in thy
sight through Jesus Christ our Lord.

Education at the time of William Scarfe

IN THE MID-NINETEENTH CENTURY, the Poor Law Comissioners for Suffolk stated that of a sample of over 1,200 paupers, only ten could read and write well, and 281 could read and write imperfectly. For all that, there is evidence to show that a certain level of literacy was more widespread than might otherwise have been believed and that those who 'signed' documents with a cross were not always incapable of reading the document or writing their own name.

How did William Scarfe learn to read and write? Clearly we shall never know the answer. Whether he learned as a child (attending day school or Sunday school) or as an adult is unclear. However, there is evidence to show that literacy in the Cosford area of Suffolk was higher than elsewhere in the county.

George III stated that it was his wish that every child in the dominion should be taught to read the Bible. With this aim, the small number of schools that existed in 1800 grew over the next fifty years.

At the turn of that century, the majority of day schools were small private establishments, though several villages around Thorpe had schools from earlier times. Felsham is known to have

Part of the diary of William Scarfe. Despite his limited education, he displays a basic competence in arithmetic and written English.

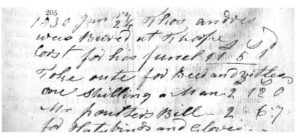

had a day school and a Sunday school as early as 1818. Drinkstone, Rattlesden and Bradfield St George had a history of educating their poor. In fact, at Bradfield, where William Scarfe grew up, four poor boys a year were chosen to be educated at Rougham under the bequest of Thomas Sparke from 1720.

Sunday schools, and evening classes for adults expanded greatly during the period leading up to 1851, as did public day schools, and by 1851 the majority of children in Suffolk received at least some education. Much of this was in crumbling buildings, conducted by ill-qualified and poorly paid teachers (often earning less than a farm labourer).

The census for 1851 lists nearly 15% of the population of Cosford hundred as scholars, which would indicate that most children between 5 and 10 attended school of some kind, though it was known that absenteeism was high, especially in country districts.

In the Church School Inquiry of 1848, amongst the most poorly funded schools were listed those at Bradfield St George, Bildeston, Drinkstone, Hitcham, Rattlesden, Rushbrooke, Stanningfield and Little Whelnetham. Though we have no early records of a school at Thorpe Morieux, a National School was built in 1844 and a Sunday School existed in 1818. Earlier foundations at Brettenham and Felsham were regarded by 1848 as the poorest of Dame Schools. John Glyde, in his book *Suffolk in the Nineteenth Century* condemns both church and gentry for their lack of financial support in founding and supporting education in their parishes; he shows that for every shilling spent on education, five shillings was being spent on the punishment of crime and the supporting of pauperism.

The causes of death in the 19th century

IN THE 1840S, CONSUMPTION (T.B.) was the main killer, claiming 23%. Diseases of old age and general decline brought about the deaths of significant numbers. About 15% died from infectious diseases – scarlatina, typhus, measles, whooping cough, diarrhoea and influenza being the main epidemics. Smallpox and cholera were less common, in spite of the fact that fewer than a quarter of all children were vaccinated. About 8% died from respiratory causes, a similar number from nervous system diseases and 6% from digestive disorders. One in twelve deaths was in the first few hours, days or weeks of life, a problem recognised even then as due to 'debility through bad nursing'.

In spite of the dangers of childbirth, women on average outlived men. Male infants were far more vulnerable than their female counterparts – about 12% died in their first year of life. For all that, about 150 people in every thousand in rural Suffolk attained an age of 75 years or more.

Fairs at the time of William Scarfe

FOR CENTURIES, VILLAGES AND TOWNS of Suffolk had hosted fairs. William Scarfe in his journal mentions a number of local ones – those at Felsham, Woolpit, Cockfield, Lavenham and Bury St Edmunds. In spite of being notorious for attracting thieves and vagabonds, they were a tremendous magnet to the working folk of Suffolk. Writing in the *Bury and Suffolk Standard* sixty years later, an anonymous contributor looked back with fondness on visiting Bury Fair as a young man. The complete article runs to several thousand words, but this edited version gives a flavour of what it must have been like to go to the fair in 1826.

Few people there are, in this year of grace, who do not go to fairs, though old ladies of nervous temperament will be afraid to venture out in the streets for fear of the *'waterloo bang-ups,'* which every urchin carries.

Along the entire west and north sides of the spacious area, from the front of the Assembly rooms to the bottom of Northgate Street, and again on to Mustow Street, stretch the *'squares'* – long canvas-covered rows of stalls on either hand of the itinerant merchants, the booths and caravans of the show people, and the stages, ups-and-downs, round-abouts, and other multiform belongings of the fraternity who in some way or other cater for the amusement of the fair-going public.

Near Mrs Gould's house at the north west corner of the hill are the round-abouts, a source of much amusement to boys and girls, who are invited by the proprietor, a red faced, greasy-coated individual, with red hair and a dusky voice to *'come and 'ave a ride, only a ha'penny a piece on the fine new helegant hosses and kerridges,'* the steeds and vehicles alluded to being wooden horses and small wooden carts mounted on the circular frame, and presenting as dingy and greasy an appearance as their owner.

The first object which captures my eye is a large red strip of canvas with some inscription upon it in very black letters, and which is fixed upon two poles, each of which is upheld by a dirty, ragged-looking boy. Approaching the canvas, I read – *'here may be obtained all the true and horrible particulars of the murder of Mr. Weare with many interesting prints relating to the murderer and his victim.'*

Among the literary ware on one stall, I see the *'History of the Wickham Skeith Wizard,'* which records how a man in that Suffolk Village, after being accused of, and persecuted for Witchcraft, was finally *'swam for a Wizard'* in the large pond on Wickham Green last July twelvemonth, in the presence of hundreds of people.

Here a wretched looking women with two children, is shrieking forth a doleful ballad: and here a fellow whose rags barely cover his nakedness is standing by a short piece of stick set upright in the ground, and upon which rests a small tin box. *'Who'll 'ave a shy for a ha'penny at a bacca box full o' ha'pence?'* he is shouting out lustily to a scant audience composed of a girl with a baby, a few little urchins and a butcher's lad.

Groups of inquisitive children are examining the backs of booths and peeping in awe through the chinks of the vans comprising Atkins's Menagerie, or scattering in terror at the sound of the lions' roars.

Fighting his way through the crowd comes a tall man crying the account of a *wonderful apparition* seen last week in Ipswich. He sells his papers right and left, and will evidently realise a pretty harvest by the end of the day. To-morrow, this knave will be elsewhere – for he knows better than to stop too long in any one place.

Oysters sellers are here, conspicuous and vociferous, chiefly in the vicinity of Abbeygate Street: the delicious bivalves are among the cheap luxuries of the poorer classes. These are washed down by draughts of Burton, Windsor or Edinburgh ale, while the ladies of the company will generally favour ginger beer and spruce in the way of liquids. The lovers of fried sausages are already patronising Baily's booth, which fronts the east side of the hill. *'The primest smoking hot sausages and the finest ales sold here,'* reads the notice over the doorway. A few yards away, is a table arranged where the board reads: *'this is the famous old Peas-pudding shop, 4d each, smoking hot, from Snow-hill, London.'*

In these and kindred places, alas, the money earned in the late harvest will melt like snow in the sun: and the lesson of last April, which was a month of unparalleled suffering, of most disastrous poverty, in thousands of homes of the working classes throughout the country, will be forgotten.

Outside Richardson's theatre, a tragic-comical company are this afternoon playing *'Paul Pry'* – the comedy with which Liston has been taking the town by storm. Among all the shows at Bury contending for popular favour, our old friend *Punch* – who of all the street exhibitions stands at the head in point of popularity – never fails to secure a mirthful and appreciative audience.

Last night at the Assembly rooms took place one of the three grand balls which are held every October during Bury fair and the large numbers of residents in the town, who during the last hour or so have found their way to the Angel Hill, have been attracted hither by what is unquestionably one of the chief sights of the fair. The grand company of aristocracy now staying in the town, who attended the ball last night, will presently, as is the custom, promenade the *'squares,'* take a view of the above – even patronizing two or three of the superior ones.

Atkins's menagerie is now *'quite full'* as the proprietor proudly announces from the stage. Here, on a line with Atkins's is the *'Queen of the Tight Rope,'* giving the public a specimen of her art and a liberal view of her understanding, which is certainly enlightened by lamps and torches innumerable.

I have just paid a visit to the booth of the *'Fire King,'* a gentleman who during the present fair has made some considerable stir by his so-called marvellous feats. He is an undoubted son of Erin and of the lowest class. He made his appearance from behind a screen in a partially nude condition, and began his performance by eating phosphorus, taking it from an iron tray and apparently enjoying it. His next refreshment was some

arsenic, which was fused over charcoal in the presence of the spectators to convince them that it *was* arsenic, but the quantity taken was evidently remarkably small. He then swallowed what the proprietor of the show declared to be oxalic acid! and finally Prussic acid! Having thus '*made a hearty meal,*' as the proprietor expressed it, a red hot iron, which had been heated at the stove, was applied to the performer's skin, when tongues of flame ran all over the exposed parts of his body in a truly alarming manner, and he was very literally '*on fire.*' The screams of the women among the spectators were presently silenced by the disappearance of the flames, and by the calmness of the performer, who was evidently unhurt in the least by the fiery ordeal through which he had passed. He concluded his exploits by plunging his hands and arms into the fire, and drawing them forth again no whit the worse.

When this festival, perchance shall live only as a memory, the faithful historian may be able to write lovingly of '*the fun and frolic of Bury Fair.*'

Crime
in the early 1800s

THERE WAS A MASSIVE RISE in the level of crime during the nineteenth century. Whilst the population grew by 56% in Suffolk between 1801 and 1851, recorded crime was up by 200%. Surprisingly, the greatest rises were in the country, not in the town. Nevertheless, most crime that came to court was trivial, as is shown by the following table.

TOTAL COMMITMENTS FOR CRIME IN SUFFOLK
1848–1852

Murder	13
Attempted murder etc.	30
Manslaughter	10
Concealing the birth of infants	9
Offences against nature	10
Rape etc.	23
Assaults	100
Other offences against the person	4
Burglary and housebreaking	113
Breaking into shops and warehouses	28
Robbery and assault with intent	43
Extortion	1
Horse and sheep stealing	52
Larceny in houses and from the person	92
Larceny by servants	198
Simple larceny	1,639
Embezzlement	46
Receiving stolen goods	81
Fraud	52
Other offences of simple theft	34
Arson	62
Killing and maiming cattle	5
Other malicious offences	7
Forgery	11
Passing counterfeit coin	18
Offences against the game laws	26
Perjury	5
Breach of the peace and riot	18
Other offences	6

Males outnumbered females in court by about 8 to 1, and most crime was commited by those under 30. The governor of Bury gaol, Patrick McIntyre stated: 'Those from populous places are profligate and drunken; from more rural places they manifest the first great want of training, idleness.' The chaplain to the gaol, Rev. W. Wells, testified to the mass of the inmates being 'little more than children, not hardened in crime, but who, from the culpable neglect of their parents, or the want of religious and moral influence at home, have gradually acquired habits of petty thieving which are connived at rather than punished by their parents'. John Glyde in *Suffolk in the Nineteenth Century* furnishes evidence that shows the Cosford hundred, and the parish of Brettenham in particular, had the highest proportion of criminality in the county.

A large amount of crime appears to have gone undetected. Of those accused that came to court, 77% were found guilty, and most received a short custodial sentence. During the period 1827–42 when most of William Scarfe's journal was written, serious crime was rare. Only 12 people were hanged in Suffolk during those 15 years (four for murder, four for arson, three for violent burglary and one for 'an unatural offence'). Countless were condemmed to death during that time, only to have their sentence commuted to one of transportation.

Lesser courts handled the most trivial of offences. In 1848, there were 97 convictions for poaching in the Bury district alone. This was often viewed as a first offence that could set felons on a slippery slope to worse crimes.

The link between pauperism and crime is throughly researched in John Glyde's book. The vast majority of adult males in Thorpe Morieux and the surrounding district are listed in the 1851 census as agricultural labourers. Their wages would probably have been about 8 shillings a week, and for three or four months of the year they may have been unemployed. As a result, their diet consisted almost entirely of bread, cheese, vegetables, tea and beer. Meat was seldom on the menu, unless illegally acquired. Mr Scott, the relieving officer for Lavenham during the 1840s, published a balance sheet which refers to Robert Crick, a local farm labourer, who may have been related to the family William Scarfe often quotes in his journal.

INCOME				EXPENDITURE		

INCOME

	age	earnings	
		s	d
Robert Crick	42	9	0
Wife	40	0	9
Boy	12	2	0
Boy	11	1	0
Girl			6
Boy			4
TOTAL		**13**	**9**

EXPENDITURE

	s	d
Bread	9	0
Potatoes	1	0
Rent	1	2
Tea	0	2
Sugar	0	3½
Soap	0	3
Blue	0	0½
Thread &c.	0	2
Candles	0	3
Salt	0	0½
Coal & wood	0	9
Butter	0	4½
Cheese	0	3
TOTAL	**13**	**9**

The margin between feeding the family and falling into debt was exceedingly tight. At this time, when local parish priests were in receipt of up to £1,000 per annum, it was not uncommon for labourers' children to be employed from the age of six or seven to bring in a few pence to swell the starving family's purse. Poverty drove many to see no sin in helping themselves to vegetables from the fields, or game from the woods.

Index

(Figures in italics denote pages with illustrations)

Absen, Mr 87
accidental deaths 20, 26–7, 38, 40, 48, 56, 65–6, 68, 136, 137, 142, 144
ague 29, 33, 88
Alderton, Ann 75
Alderton, Harriet 30–1
Alderton, Herbert Edward 75
Alderton, John 144
Alderton, Robert 30, 144
Alderton, *see also* Allington
Allen, Elizabeth 167
Allington, Benjamin 30
Allington, Elizabeth: leaves Bradfield Manger 143; marries 143–4
Allington, Elizabeth (diarist's mother-in-law), dies 160
Allington, Fred 133
Allington, Frederick 109, 110, 152
Allington, Harriet 30–1
Allington, John 143; marries 143–4
Allington, Joseph, born 30
Allington, Joseph (diarist's brother-in-law) 23, 26, 109; dies 114
Allington, Mary 162; seeks bastardy

order 74–6
allotments 112, *113*
amputation 130, *131*
Anderson, Rev. Thomas 45, 46, 92; sells Glebe Grove 131
Andrews, George 78; steals cheeses 25, 28; sells pigs 44
Andrews, John, dies 109
Andrews, Robert, his bread stolen 125
Andrews, Thomas: taken ill 57–8; dies 58; buried 60
Andrews, Thomas (boy), injured 68
Angel Inn 82
apple scions 78
Arbon, Mr 87
Arbon, Susan, dies 107
Arnold, John, dies 152
arson 67
Atkins' menagerie 174
Aves, Joseph: sells horse 61; marries 121
Aves, Martha, dies 110
Aves, Thomas, dies 19
Avis, Azariah, marries 127

bacon 67
Baldwin, Mary, dies 53, 68
Baldwin, Samuel: liaison with Susan
Snell 68–9; marries 71
Baldwin, William, hangs himself 85
ball, Mr Kinsey's 57
banknotes 82
baptism, age at 88
bark 98; peeling *4,* 90, 99, 117, 121,
126, 136, 145, 147; use in tanning
99, 116
Barrell, Isaac 90
bastardy 30, 40, 71, 75–6, 107, 135
Bear public house 82
beating the bounds 25
beer 55
bees 137
bell-ringing 29
Benefit Clubs 59
Bernard, Ann 167
Beyton 82, 141
Bildeston 61, *62,* 70, 141; school 172
Billingford House, barn struck by
lightning 110
Bird, Bet, marries 108, 109
Bird, John: Susan Snell leaves him
68; as woodman 77, 99, 145, 147;
remarries 85; moves house 87; dies
132
Bird, Kerenhappuck: taken ill 55–6,
61; dies 64
Bixby, Elizabeth, dies 91, 114
Bixby, Jemima, marries 55
bladder stones 62
Blumfield, George, dies 143
Bogges *see* Boggies
Boggies, Charlotte 119
Boggies, Emily, born 118
Boggies, Frances, marries 41
Boggies, George: marries 115; his son
born 119

Boggies, James 44, 45, 102, 132; dies
136
Boggies, James junior 118
Boggies, Maria 118, 162; *see also*
Scarfe, Maria
Boggies, May, dies 132
Boggies, Mrs, godmother to Jacob
Scarfe 104
Boggies, Sarah, taken ill 28
Boggies, wife of James junior, dies
115
Boggies, William, born 119
Boggis *see* Boggies
Borley, Hannah, dies 45
boundary stone 91
boxing 91, 101
Bradfield Combust 92, 133, 144
Bradfield Lodge 57
Bradfield Manger 91–2, 133, 143–4
Bradfield St Clare, church *19*
Bradfield St George 158; education
in 172
Bradfield Wood 50, 64; coppicing *41*
Bramford, John, imprisoned for theft
98
Brandon 82
brashing *see* brushing
Brettenham: Scott's house 87; beer-
house 90; prize fight 91; school
172; *see also* Ryece Hall
Brettenham Hall *81,* 83
Brettenham Meeting 64
Brewer, Susannah, dies 45
Brick Kiln Cottages 127
brick kilns 127
Brighton, Robert, drowned 27
Brinkley, Samuel, dies 152
Briton School 145
Brook Hall *43,* 47
brotches *100,* 106
Brown, Lisa 103

Brundish Friendly Society 155
brushing 108, 109, 117, 125, 136, 145, 149
brushwood *94, 108*
Buckmaster family 42
Bunbury, Sir Henry 112, 129
Bury St Edmunds: fair 25, *49, 50,* 174–7; gaol 26, 36, *69*, 71, 86, 178–9; hospital 45, 62, *63*
Buxhall Mill 92

Cadge, John, dies 144–5
Cadge, Sarah, remarries 145
Cahusac, Frank Hamilton 166
Camac, Henrietta, buried 81
Candlemas 155
Carpenter, Marielena, buried 132
Carter, Henry, dies 48
carts 48, 69, 78, 92, 95, 105, 118; *see also* waggons
Chapman, John 165
charcoal *80*
charity 22, 32, 43, 53, 54, 71, 107
chicken-pox 57
Chinery, Abraham 126
Chinery, Mrs, visits diarist 135
Clark, Mrs 61
Clarke, John, marries Ann 29
Clarke, Susan, gives birth 31
Clarke, William, baptised 31
Clements, Ann, marries 29
Clements, Edward 43, 47
Clements, Robert, robbed of wheat 69
Clements, Samuel 65
clothing 22, 31, 37, 44–5
coal 118
coats 22, 37
Cockfield: church tower 20, *21*; fair 91; Hall 38; unlawful assembly 71–2
Cockfield Green 20
Codd, Edwin, marries 66

cold weather 51, 54
Cole, Rev. Mr, 25, 32
Combs Tannery *116*
Combs Wood *94*
confirmations 23, 141
constables 71
Cook, Charles, marries 61
Cook, Elizabeth, death 26
Copford Hall 90, *146*
coppicing *41*, 50, 64, *94, 98*
Corder, William: and Red Barn murder 34–6; body dissected 62
Cornell, George 29
corning frolic 132
coronation 137–40
court baron 53
Cousens, James, imprisoned after trespassing 43–4
Crick, Charles, dies 33
Crick, Edward 22–3; his daughter born 49; as woodman 77, 136, 145, 147; diarist pays him wages for his boy 102; supplies coal 118
Crick, Elizabeth 25
Crick, Frederick, born 115
Crick, George, named 141
Crick, Henry, dies 33
Crick, John, dies 22
Crick, Mary: dies 115; marries 121
Crick, Robert 179–80
Crick, Sarah, born 49
Crick, Sarah (triplet), dies 33
Crick, Susan: gives birth 32, 44, 49, 87; pregnant 95
Crick, Tom 136
Crick, Walter, born 87
crime 177–9; *see also* fraud; poaching; theft
Croker, Rev. Mr 61
Cudbard, Hannah, marries 70
Cullum, arrested for robbery 143

Dalton, John 62
Dalton, Sarah, dies 44
Darby, William 48
Dasely, Rev. Mr 60
Davers, Charles 103
Davers, Rev. Robert 103
Day, William, taken for robbery
124–5
Deacon, Elizabeth *see* Scarfe,
Elizabeth
death: causes 173; (particular
instances) 22, 49, 53, 66, 73, 85,
87, 90, 95, 102, 107, 123, 132, 133,
136, 144, 153; *see also* accidental
death; infant mortality; suicide
Debenham, Charles 74–5
debt 44–5, 179–81
Decarle, John Parkenson, dies 40
Dedman, William, remarries 75
Deeks 165
Diggins, Ann, buried 65
dining 46
Diss, mill 110
doctors 61, 80, 115, 118, 151
Drinkstone 172
drunkenness 90, 95
Dyer, William, fathers a bastard 107

Edge, Peter 166
education 171–2
Edwardstone 88
elections 129
Eley, M. 37
Eley, Mary Anne, marries 137
Ellis family, of Bury 50
Elsden, Edward 156
Ely, Newport and Elizabeth 25
Esling, John, dies 136
Estling, Amelia, dies 142
Estling, John, dies 152
Euston 88–9

eye operations 118
Faires, George 45
fairs 25, 48, *49*, 50, 67, 82, 88, 91,
110, 143, 149, 174–7
Farnley, Ann, dies 115
Farnley, Samuel 69; sells flour 46;
dies 84; house sold to Scarfe 104
fast days 88
fathoms 116
felling 83, 84, 94, 110, 117
Felsham: church *29*; church gate *47*;
fair 48, 67, 149; school 172; *see
also* Six Bells
Felsham Club 24–5, 45, 58, 61, 75–7,
85, 103, 109, 136, 141, 149, 151;
feast 152; *see also under* Scarfe,
William (the diarist)
Felsham Hall Wood *see* Bradfield
Wood
Felsham Wood 50, 75, 83, 94, 110,
115, 117, 136; aerial photo *120*
fever 30, 102, 107; *see also* ague
fires 31–2, 42, 67, 92, 142
Fiske family 166
Fiske, John 166
Fiske, John junior 166
Fiske, Sarah Thomas 167
flooding 27, 60–1
flour, price 147
Folly Farm 64, 85, 103, 104, 109
food 179–80; *see also* dining
Fornham 79
Fox public house 88–9
fraud 82
Friendly Societies 24, 58, 59, 103, 155
frolics 107
frost 135
funerals 58, 75–7; sermons 50, 60,
103, 147; expenses 60, 85, 165

Gardiner, Mary, dies 58

Garnham, Mrs: her property burnt
down 31; and rebuilt 34, 42; farm
supplies pig 87
gates 149
Gault, Mrs 61
Gault, William, dies 30
Gedding, riots 70
Gennet, Mead 23, 26
George IV, King, dies 67
gin 47
Gladwell, John 131
Gladwell, William, of Felsham, dies 88
Gladwell, William, of Rattlesden 131
Glebe Grove 131
Glyde, John 172, 179
Goldsmith, T. 27
Goodwin, Robert, 71
Goold, Amy, dies 67
Goold, Bixby 41
Goold, Elfred, as woodman 77, 136
Goold, Henry, creditors' sale 44
Goold, John 45; taken ill 155
Goold, Joseph 57, 58; dies 103
Goold, Sarah: dies 57; buried 58
Goold, Thomas: taken ill 147; sings at
Hessett church 148
Gosfield Park 52
Gould see Goold
Great Hastings Wood see Hastings
Wood
Green, Benjamin 91
Green, Harriet, dies 90
Green, John: argues with Samuel
Howard 68; robbed 124
Green, Margaret Darby, buried 57
Green, William 91; marries 114
Grimard, William, robbed at fair 88
Grimwade, George 79, 94
Grimwade, John, dies in infancy 65
Grimwade, Sarah Ann, dies 65
Grimwood, Henry: taken ill 56, 60;

dies 109
Grimwood, Robert, marries 152
Grove Farm 31–2, 34, 42
Growse, Robert 61, 118, 151; his
house at Bildeston 62
Gypsy (mare) 82, 104, 105, 132

Hammond, Charles, dies 64
Hammond, Elizabeth 37
Harper, Mr, of Hitcham Hall 42
Harper, Steven 91
Harrison family 166, 168
Harrison, Anne 33, 168
Harrison, Charles, dies 96
Harrison, Elizabeth, born 90
Harrison, Elizabeth (Major Harrison's
sister) 167
Harrison, Fiske Goodeve 167
Harrison, Hezekiah Goodeve 166,
167; dies 148
Harrison, John 167
Harrison, John Haynes (Major)
125–6; owns Ryece Hall 42; invites
diarist to live at Brook Hall 43;
quarrel over housekeeper 47; taken
ill 145; comes to Brook Hall 146;
buried 147; dies 148; family tree
167
Harrison, Miss, charitable giving 43
Harrison, Mrs 126
Harrison, Ralph Ward, dies 146
Harrison, Thomas Bernard 167
Harrison, Thomas Haynes 45, 167
Harrison, Rev. Thomas Thomas
166; gives prayer book to William
Scarfe 9–12, 157; charitable
giving 22, 107; marries Anne 33;
preaching 50; family tree 167;
monuments *168*
Harrison, William Thomas 166, 167,
170

harvest 47, 79, 94, 104, 105, 110, 112, 117, 121, 128, 129, 149; *see also* corning frolic

Haselwood, Matilda, dies 148

Hastings Wood 42, 50, 64, *98*, 99, 106, 108; poaching 65; aerial photo *120*

Haward, Frances 41

Haward, George: joins militia 28; marries 41

Haward, Henry, born 88

Haward, John, remarriage 33

haymaking *105*, *128*; *see also* harvest

Hayward, Maria, marries 104

Henslow, Rev. Professor 112

Hewes, Mary Ann, marries 66

Higham 95

Hill Farm 132

Hitcham, school 172

Hoddy, John, dies 65–6

holidays 67, 91

Horkings, William, dies 80

Horrex, Zechariah, dies 96

Horrex, Hannah, marries 126

horses 50, 61, 78, 82, 102, 125, 127

hospitals *see under* Bury St Edmunds

housekeepers 47

How, Francis, marries 55

How, Samuel, buys pigs 44

Howard, Eliza, dies 33

Howard, George: sells handkerchief 30; falls off waggon 44; his child dies 48; sells beer 54–5; sells pigs 77, 102, 137; pays his bill 106

Howard, Harriet, born 66–7

Howard, Henry, dies 48

Howard, James 134

Howard, John: taken ill 80; complains about behaviour of boy in church 86; hosts singing frolic 142; dies 151

Howard, Mary, dies 121

Howard, Samuel 68

Howard, Susan, marries 152

Howard, William, marries 126

Howe, Elizabeth, marries 104

Howe, Francis 61

Howlett, Edward: buys brotches 100, 106; dies 152

hulks *124*

Hunt, William, dies 66

hurdles 75, *79*, 83, *84*, 92, 123, *176*

Hustler, Charles Edward 124; sells bacon 67; sells a horse 133; dies 136

Hyam, Laurence 37, 142

illegitimate births *see* bastardy

infant mortality 173; (particular instances) 33, 48, 65, 75, 95, 96, 103, 107, 119

influenza 123, 173

itch 85

Jackson, Isaac 67

Jackson, Mr 122

Jennies, Edward, steals cheeses 25, 28

Jipsey (mare) 82, 104, 105, 132

Johnson, Henry, transported for theft 77

Jolly Boys (club) 24

Josselyn, J., of Sproughton 52, 112

Keble, Charlotte 74

kells 98

Kembel, Miss 29

Kerridge, G., robbed of barley 86

kidney stones 62

King, Thomas, diary 47, 56, 92, 110, 124

Kinsey, Sarah 25

Kinsey, Simon, steals wheat 69

Kinsey, William 25; holds a ball 57

Labourers' Friend Society 112

Lambert, William, dies 75–7

Lane, Susan, dies 142
Langham, John 144; visits diarist 155
Lansdell, Mr, robbed 143
larceny *see* theft
Last, Frances, burial 22
Last, James: loses a horse 127; taken ill 127
Last, Simon: obtains hurdles from diarist 83; barley stolen 98
Last, Thomas, rebuilds barn 34
Lavenham 139, 141, 175; fair 88, 143
Leheup, Ann, buried 105
Leheup, Michael Peter, buried 132
Levett, Benjamin, marries 104
life expectancy 108, 173; *see also* infant mortality
lightning 111, 112, 125
Lister, Elizabeth, buried 108
Lister, John, dies 87
Lister, Susan, dies 141
Lister, William: imprisoned for poaching 33, 65; remarries 108, 122; as woodman 145, 147
lits 92, 148
Little Bardfield 148
Little Whelnetham 30; school 172
Livermeere (Livermoore?) 133
Loake, John 43
Logan, Hart 129
Long, Ann, dies 127
Long, Henry, dies 22
Long, John: imprisoned for theft 26; as woodman 77, 136; dies 135
Long, Robert, imprisoned for theft 25–6, 28
Lunn, Charlotte, marries 115
Lyes, Mary Ann 135

machine-breaking 71, 72
McIntyre, Patrick 178–9
Maggs, James, diary 144

Maidwell, Thomas, dies 97
Makin, Maria-Ann, marries 114
Makings, Ann 49, 67
Makings, James, injured 152
malt kells 98
Manger public house 92, 144
manor courts 53, 148
Market Weston, church struck by lightning 110
Markham, Mr 82
marriage, age at 147
Marshall, Mr 152
Marten, Maria 34–6
Mays, Fred, prize fight 91
Melton, Amelia 119
Melton, Catherine 47
Melton, Frances 107, 119
Melton, Frederic Rands 98, 107; sells pig 87
Melton, Mary, disputes her father's will 74
Melton, Mary Ann, marries 71
Melton, Orlando, born 107
Melton, Samuel 43
midwifery 87
migration to cities 23
militia 28, 77
Miller, John Garrad 58
Milton, John, baptised 52
Moat Farm Cottage *97*, *106*, *134*, 148, *149*; aerial photograph *120*
Morgan, Benjamin, dies 107
Morgan, Elizabeth, dies 60
Morgan, Mr, his house occupied by Mr Maidwell 97
Mudd, Drinkstone 49
Mudd, Francis David, dies 115
Mudd, Frederick, dies 60
Mudd, Henry, dies 151
Mudd, Mary Ann, marries 96
Mudd, Richard 115

Mulley, John (Robert): leaves his farm 23; dies 30
Mumford, John 148
murder 34–6, 52

Nethergates, John, builds new oven 147
Newson, William 77
Nice, William 100
Nisbett, John Alexander: rents Brettenham Hall 81; dies 83
Noah, Master, killed 136
Norman, William, dies in fall from tower 20
North, John 33; as woodman 99
North, Mary 85; her child dies 95
North, Mary Ann, born 143
North, Mary Ann Sarah, dies 151
North, Thomas, dies 135
North, William: gives present to Maria 29; rebuilds barn 34; dies 49
North, William junior 53, 98; his cottage 53, *150*; sells cart to diarist 69; marries 96; born 117; supplies new window frames 141; makes gates 149
North Lopham 110
Nowton Hall 49

Offord, Hannah, dies 133
Offord, Mary, dies 73
Offord, Richard, marries 137
Offord, Susan, dies 94
Olley, William 72
Orams, Mrs 77
Orridge, John 26
Orsborn, Isaac, buried 152
Osborn, John, marries 145
Osborne, James, transported for theft 77
osier beds 101
Ousden 88–9
ovens 147

overseers' accounts 164

Pakenham mill 92
Palmer, John: marries 104; cottage *150*
Palmer, Maria, dies 151
Palmer, Sarah: baptised 104; marries 146
Palmer, William 40, 41
parish houses 58–9
Partridge, Mr 82
Payne, Anne, dies 37
Payne, Elizabeth, buried 20
Payne, Robert, marries 71
Payne, William, breaks a leg 102
pheasants 65
pigs 26, 44, 77, 78, 87, 102, 107, 137
Pilbrow, Elizabeth, dies 102
Pilbrow, Robert, dies 135
Pilbrow, Robert, the younger 55
Pilbrow, Thomas William 67; prize fight 101; dies 141
Pizzey, Mary Ann, marries 47
Pizzey, Samuel: wife dies 38; marries 47
Plume, John, dies 136
poaching 33, 65
poles *94*
poor houses 58–9, 70
Poor Law 169
Poslingford 22
poverty 53, 54, 70, 179–80; *see also* debt
Powle, Alfred, imprisoned after trespassing 43–4
Pratt, Widow 163
preaching *see* funerals, sermons
Preston 58
prison hulks *124*
prisons *see* Bury St Edmunds, gaol; hulks
prize-fights 91

pubs *see* Angel Inn; Bear; Fox;
Manger; Six Bells; White Horse
Puck, John, imprisoned for poaching 33
Purkiss, Isaac 30–1

quoit beds 101

Rafe, Mrs, dies 94
Rafe (or Raffe) family 119
Raffe, 'old Master', dies 153
rain 47, 90, 91, 144
Raker, Frederick 75
Raker, Joel 78, 80; injured 137
Raker, John 91; his horse struck by
lightning 125
Raker, Louisa, marries 152
Raker, Mr & Mrs 92, 105
Rands, Samuel, dies 74
Ranson, William, death 22
Rattlesden: militia 28; riots 70; diarist
visits 126; education in 172
Red Barn murder 34–6
Redenhall, church struck by lightning
110
remarriage of widowers 122
removal orders 159
Resbrook, Mrs, leg amputated 130
Risby, Richard, buried 83
riving 100, *101*
road accidents 38, 40, 48, 65–6, 136,
137
roads *38*
robbery 143
Roberts, John, dies 122
Rougham 172
Rush, Samuel: his cheeses stolen 25;
dies 98
Rush, Samuel junior, cart accident 118
Rush, Sarah, buried 123
Rush, William, marries 146
Rushbrock, 'young Mr' 141

Rushbrooke, school 172
Rushbrooke, Col. R. 129
Ryece Hall *42*

Sadler, James, sells pigs 107
Sadman, Mr 29
Salmon, Abraham 45
Saville, Joseph, imprisoned for
leading riot 72
Scarf *see* Scarfe
Scarfe, Elizabeth (diarist's mother)
158, 159, 162; dies 160
Scarfe, Elizabeth (granddaughter of
diarist), born 153
Scarfe, Esau 162; born 35–6; carried
to Felsham fair 48; chicken-pox
57; goes to church 90; visits John
Raker 91; wife and children 153
Scarfe family *149*, 163–5
Scarfe, Frances: suffers a stillbirth?
143; registers diarist's death 153
Scarfe, Isaac: born 35–6; carried to
Felsham fair 48; chicken-pox 57;
gets dizzy 82; goes to church 90;
visits John Raker 91
Scarfe, Isaac (diarist's grandfather)
162; funeral 165
Scarfe, Isaac (grandson of diarist) 162
Scarfe, Jacob (grandson of diarist)
162; born 102; baptised 104
Scarfe, John (diarist's father) 158,
159, 162; dies 160
Scarfe, John (grandson of diarist) *18*,
157, 162; born 160
Scarfe, John, of Hessett (brother
of diarist) 162; gives pigs to his
brother 26; wife dies 41; gives corn
to his brother 42, 53, 71; goes to
Felsham fair 48; entertains family
to dinner 65; buys diarist's cart
74; buys mare 82; visits diarist 92;

birthday 95; buys house for his
brother 97, 104; harvest 104, 105,
110, 117, 121; entertains Rakers to
dinner 105; injured 105; at Felsham
Fair 149; lip sown up 151; dies
153; born 158

Scarfe, Maria 160, 162; goes to
Felsham fair 48; buys wood 102;
tapped by doctor 118, 119; dies 119

Scarfe, Mary (diarist's wife) 156, 162;
taken ill 29, 135, 143; stays with
Mrs Bird 55–6; given a pig 78;
visits Beyton 114; dies 153; born
158

Scarfe, Mary (granddaughter of
diarist) 162; born 147

Scarfe, Mary (grandmother of diarist)
162

Scarfe, Mary (sister-in-law of diarist):
dies 41; buried 42

Scarfe, Matilda (diarist's daughter),
dies 160

Scarfe, Mrs, of Felsham 44

Scarfe, Mrs John 123

Scarfe, Susannah 153

Scarfe, Walter 163

Scarfe, William (diarist's grandson)
162; born 78

Scarfe, William (diarist's son) 162;
as woodman 50; sworn in as
constable 70; helps with harvest 79;
moves into cottage with his father
106; remarries 121; helps with
haymaking 128; born 160

Scarfe, William (the diarist):
receives gift of prayer book 9–12,
157; receives gift of pigs from
brother 26; buys silk handkerchief
30; buys waistcoat 31; buys great
coat 37, 142; receives corn from his
brother 42, 53, 71; declines position

at Brook Hall 43; buys pigs 44, 77,
87, 102, 107, 137; as woodman
50, 77, 90, 92, 94, 98, 99, 108,
114, 117, 125, 126, 136, 145, 147,
149; hurts his throat 63; goes to
Brettenham Meeting 64; buys cart
69; sworn in as constable 70; sells
cart to his brother 74; buys apple
scions 78; his cart broken 78–9; his
horses 78, 82, 104, 132, 133; helps
with harvest 79, 94, 104, 105, 110,
117, 128, 129, 149; takes coals to
Hessett 80; tithe assessment 83–4;
house bought for him 97, 104, *106*,
118; goes to Felsham Church 98,
141; and Felsham Club 103, 151,
152, 155; argues with John Stearn
106–7; singing 107, 126, 141, 142,
148; cart accident 118; thatches
his house 121; visits Joseph Aves
121; visits Abraham Chinery 126;
votes 129; buys the Glebe Grove
131; goes to Hessett 141; buys
hat 142; has new oven made 147;
enters his house in court rolls 148;
sings at Hessett church 148; loses
his strength 151; dies 153; death
certificate *154*; born 158; family
tree 162; funeral 165; education
171–2

Scarff *see* Scarfe

Scarpe *see* Scarfe

Scarph *see* Scarf

schools 169–70

Scott, Charles, marries 135

Scott, Elizabeth, dies 66

Scott, Harriet, her child ill 142

Scott, of Lavenham 175

seeding 117

Semer 125

Semer Hill 136

sermons *see* funerals, sermons
settlement of paupers 158
Seyman, Battley, marries 70
Sharman, Pearson 53, 104
Shouldham Fair 82
Shrovetide fair 88
Sicklesmere 30
singing frolics 107, 126–7, 133, 142
Six Bells public house 24, 25, 33, 47,
    152; ball at 57
skating 56
smallpox 77, 171
Smith, Amy, marries 127
Smith, Benjamin 77, 87
Smith, Elizabeth, buried 63
Smith, James, dies 85
Smith, John 72
Smith, Mary Ann, dies 63
Smith, Mrs, her dairy robbed 125
Smith, Samuel 72
Smith, Thomas 103; buried 151
Smith, William 165
Snell, Charles, dies 149
Snell, Frances, marries 121
Snell, Hannah 40
Snell, Liza, comes to Thorpe 133
Snell, Louisa, baptised 41
Snell, Lucy 41
Snell, Sophia, baptised 41
Snell, Susan 68–9; marries 71
Snell, William, marries 40
Snell, 'young' 124
Snelling, Robert Hunt 69
snow 51, 56, 60, 64, 71, 75, 85, 91,
    96, 121, 122, 124, 133, 134, 135,
    142, 143, 144, 146
South Harsted 52
Southgate, Robert, killed 144
Spark(e), James, dies 114
Spark(e), Sarah, dies 106
Spark(e), Thomas 40, 87; sells house

97; sells pigs 102; dies 133
Sparrow family 50, 52, 123, 166
Sparrow, Henry 112
Sparrow, James Goodeve 52
Sparrow, John 166
Sparrow, Joseph 166
Spink, Henry, marries 152
Spite, Isaac, robbed 143
Stanningfield, school 172
steam packets 110, *111*
Stearn, Hannah, dies 50
Stearn, Harriett, marries 135
Stearn, John 86, 103, 106–7, 129,
    132; plans coronation feast 138–40
Stearn, Joseph 95
Stearne, Edward 148
steeples 20, 110
Stevens, Jonathan, dies 88
Stiff, Susan, dies 151
storms *see* tempests
Stow Lodge 44, *45*
Stowmarket 118
Sturgeon, Mrs William, dies 133
Sturgeon, Sarah 74
Sturgeon, William 91–2; buried 151
Subbings, James 148
suicide 85, 88, 141
Sunday schools 171–2
surgeons 118, 151; *see also* doctors
Sutton, Abraham, moves house 49
Sutton (man injured) 68
swindlers 82
Swing Riots 70, 71, 72, *73*
Symonds, Daniel 85–6
Symonds, Thomas 85–6
Symons, 'young' 121

Talbott, John, dies 38
tanneries *116*
Tasmania 125
Tate, William, transported for theft 77

Taylor, Amy 74
Taylor, John, dies 38
Taylor, Robert: his property burnt down 31–2; and rebuilt 34, 42; moves to Ryece Hall 42
Taylor, Sarah: marries 61; dies 85
Taylor, Webb, imprisoned after trespassing 43–4
Taylor, William 71–2
tempests 46, 92, 110, 121, 125
Temple, Robert Charles 166
thatching 100, 121
theft 25, 41, 43–4, 58, 69, 77, 85–6, 88, 124–5
Thelnetham 92
Thorpe Hall 52
Thorpe Morieux: church 119, 168; Rectory 134; Rectors 166–9; schools 172: see also Folly Farm; Moat Farm Cottage; Valley Farm
Thorpe Wood 50, 90, 92, 95, 114, 117, 121, 125, 136, 145, 148, 149; aerial photo 120
threshing machines 68
Thurston 28
tithe 83–4
tithe-feasts 38
Todd, George, prize fight 101
Tomlinson, Ann 167
Tomlinson, Anne, marries 33
Tracey, John, hospital operation 62
Tracey, Mrs, taken ill 107
Tracey, Robert: gets drunk 90; ill 107
transportation 72, 77, 124, 179
Travers Fair 110
treadmill 86
trespassing 43–4
tuberculosis 48, 173
Tweed, John 45; buried 149
urban migration 23

Valley Farm 31–2, 34, 42
Vince, Martha, dies 62
wages 70, 102, 136, 179–80
waggons 65–6, 87, 136, 144, 152; see also carts
waistcoats 31
Walpole, William 102
Walton, Thomas 57
Waterman, of Brettenham 98
Wattisham: Meeting House 37; riots 70
Wayman, John 20
weather see cold weather; flooding; frost; lightning; rain; snow; tempests
weddings, dates of 122
Wells, W. 174
Wenyeve family 81
Wheelwrights (cottage) 53, 54, 150
White, Charles, dies 141
White Horse public house 82
Whitsunday 91
widows, remarriage 33, 122
Wilding, William, dies 122
Wilkinson, Hannah 40
William IV, King: accession 66; crowned 67
Wilson, Henry 129
window frames 141
Wittel, Lydia, marries 85
Woodbridge, damage by lightning 112
woodland management 50
Woods, arrested for robbery 143
Woolpit 127; fair 82
workhouses: Stowmarket 44; Semer 125
Wright, John, buried 47
Wyard, William, imprisoned after trespassing 43–4
Wythe, arrested for robbery 143
York, Duke of, death 19